HSC

**DO NOT REMOVE
CARDS FROM POCKET**

GET YOUR CAR
FIXED FREE

MORT SCHULTZ

and the Editors of
Consumer Reports Books

CONSUMER REPORTS BOOKS
A Division of Consumers Union
Yonkers, New York

Published by Consumers Union of United States, Inc.,
Yonkers, New York 10703.

Library of Congress Cataloging-in-Publication Data

Schultz, Morton J.
    Get your car fixed free / by Mort Schultz and the editors of
Consumer Reports Books.
        p. cm.
    ISBN 0-89043-627-4
    1. Automobiles—United States—Maintenance and repair.
    2. Warranty—United States.   I. Consumer Reports Books.   II. Title.
TL 152.S386   1994
629.28'72—dc20   94-9047
                                                                      CIP

Design by GDS/Jeffrey L. Ward

First printing, July 1994

This book is printed on recycled paper. ♻

Manufactured in the United States of America

Get Your Car Fixed Free is a Consumer Reports Book published by Consumers Union, the nonprofit organization that publishes *Consumer Reports*, the monthly magazine of test reports, product Ratings, and buying guidance. Established in 1936, Consumers Union is chartered under the Not-for-Profit Corporation Law of the State of New York.

The purposes of Consumers Union, as stated in its charter, are to provide consumers with information and counsel on consumer goods and services, to give information on all matters relating to the expenditure of the family income, and to initiate and to cooperate with individual and group efforts seeking to create and maintain decent living standards.

Consumers Union derives its income solely from the sale of *Consumer Reports* and other publications. In addition, expenses of occasional public service efforts may be met, in part, by nonrestrictive, noncommercial contributions, grants, and fees. Consumers Union accepts no advertising or product samples and is not beholden in any way to any commercial interest. Its Ratings and reports are solely for the use of the readers of its publications. Neither the Ratings, nor the reports, nor any Consumers Union publications, including this book, may be used in advertising or for any commercial purpose. Consumers Union will take all steps open to it to prevent such uses of its material, its name, or the name of *Consumer Reports*.

CONTENTS

INTRODUCTION

THE TITLE OF THIS BOOK IS CORRECT. ONCE YOU know how to go about it, the chances are likely that you'll be able to have repairs made to your vehicle for free or on a shared basis with the manufacturer.

A skeptic might ask, "Since when have manufacturers become so altruistic that they'll fix cars for nothing? Or have you, the author, devised some formula that can force a manufacturer to pay totally or partially for a repair?"

Neither. In all but one aspect, which will be discussed, what's described in this book should come as no surprise to someone who has read the owner's manual and/or the warranty information disclosure material that accompanies every vehicle, new or used.

Part I of this book discusses the significance of the hundreds of service advisories issued annually by car manufacturers to the service departments of dealerships that sell their products. These service advisories, which are called "secret warranties" by some, tell dealership mechanics how to make repairs and install newly modified parts, eliminating problems brought on by original parts. As you will find out when you read Part I, service advisories don't apply only to brand-new vehicles. Many of them are issued two or three years after a model has been on the road. Some are issued to cover cars that were manufactured even as long as ten years before the publication date of the service advisory.

Obviously, a manufacturer doesn't advertise the existence of service advisories. To do so would be to admit to flaws in design or in the manufacturing process. But when a manufacturer is confronted by an owner with a document confirming that a car problem is the fault of the manufacturer, he usually has no recourse but to repair the problem described in the service advisory at no cost to the customer, even though all warranties have expired.

Part II and Part III describe the significance of federal safety and emissions recall laws that require manufacturers to repair thousands of defective vehicles each year at no cost to owners. Free repairs that are made to rectify a safety or emissions system defect often fix other problems resulting from the existence of the safety or emissions deficiency. Owners who don't recognize this may end up paying for a repair they could have had made for free.

It should also come as no surprise to a new car owner that vehicles are accompanied by warranties that extend beyond the basic period of 12 months or 12,000 miles, whichever comes first. Some of these "extra" warranties can cover your car for as much as 100,000 miles. Two "extra" warranties, which are required by federal law, cover vehicles that are sold by new and used car dealers against emissions control deficiencies for as long as five years or 50,000 miles, whichever occurs first. As detailed in Part IV, these deficiencies usually cause other problems that owners don't relate to an emissions control defect.

No matter what your situation, never take a dealer's word that you aren't entitled to a free or shared-cost repair. Remember, dealers don't pay for repairs: Manufacturers do. If you run into an obstinate dealer, take your case to the manufacturer. When presented with proof that shows that you have a valid argument, a manufacturer will generally repair the vehicle for free.

PART I

Getting Your Car Fixed Free
by Uncovering

A SECRET WARRANTY

Secret Warranty! This Insidious-Sounding phrase, coined by the media, describes inherent problems that vehicle manufacturers don't make public. These problems develop when less-than-adequate components are installed in cars, light trucks, vans, and utility vehicles or when there is a deficiency in the manufacturing process.

An inherent car problem is acknowledged by a manufacturer in an advisory—usually in the form of a technical service bulletin (TSB)—issued to dealer service departments describing how to make the repair. Advisories can also take the form of private letters. This method, however, is rarely used anymore because it's frowned on by government agencies like the National Highway Traffic Safety Administration (NHTSA) and by states that have passed or are threatening passage of anti–secret warranty legislation.

Unfortunately, inherent problems often are not discovered until new vehicle warranties have expired. Therefore, car owners may not have a clue that the problems they are experiencing are caused by manufacturing flaws. Car owners can be left holding the bag for the cost of repairs.

Repairing inherent defects normally involves installing newly designed components or making adjustments. Most repairs average about one hour to perform, and the cost is usually less than $200.

However, some inherent defects can be repaired only by overhauling an engine, rebuilding a transmission or differential, replacing expensive parts of a steering or braking system, or repainting a vehicle. Then the cost can run into the thousands.

ROLE OF THE FEDERAL GOVERNMENT

Federal law requires that service bulletins acknowledging deficiencies in the manufacture of vehicles be sent to the NHTSA, which is an agency of the U.S. Department of Transportation. But under federal law, no one else has to be notified, not even the car owners or independent or franchised repair shops. As much as the law allows, service bulletins are kept secret from everyone except dealers selling vehicles from a particular manufacturer.

This part of *Get Your Car Fixed Free* deals with getting your hands on a secret warranty to prove that the problem you're having with your vehicle is the fault of the manufacturer, so that you can have the trouble fixed free, especially if your new car warranty has expired.

START OF SECRET WARRANTIES

The service bulletin system was started somewhere around 1915 by Henry Ford. It was established to support the first nationwide dealership program that Ford set up to sell and service the Model T, which was the first mass-produced car in the United States.

At the time, Ford decided that some method was needed to keep mechanics in his dealerships apprised of the most up-to-date troubleshooting and repair information. The service bulletin program he started was so successful that it was adopted by all manufacturers and prevails to this day.

From the beginning, service bulletins have been kept secret. Before a federal law was passed requiring manufacturers to send bulletins to NHTSA, no one other than car dealers received them, except for selected individuals such as some members of the media.

Therefore today, when trouble develops with a car, light truck, van, or utility vehicle because of an inherent defect after expiration of the warranty, odds are that the owner will pay to have it fixed.

Over the years, limited distribution of service bulletins has caused another headache for vehicle owners. Since repairs devised by manufacturers are known only to dealership mechanics, getting a proper repair from an independent or franchised mechanic has been a hit-or-miss proposition. One reason for not giving these repair shops the latest repair information is to pressure car owners to patronize service departments of new car dealers.

THE HIGH NUMBER OF INHERENT DEFECTS

Manufacturers usually send TSBs to dealers once a week or once every two weeks. The number of problems that are acknowledged as being inherent by these documents is amazing. In 1993 alone, Ford, General Motors, and Chrysler issued an average of 300 service bulletins each—Honda/Acura, Nissan, and Toyota a lesser number. Most bulletins describe how to repair inherent problems, but not all. Others tell dealership mechanics how to service newly developed components or relate information important only to dealer service departments, such as time/labor allowances.

For most TSBs, defects that are acknowledged as inherent apply to a limited number of vehicles, usually only several thousand. Therefore, be prepared to hear a service manager say that a given bulletin you know about doesn't apply to your vehicle. However, that bulletin may reveal a repair that you've been looking to make since the car was purchased. On the other hand, the number of cars, light trucks, vans, and utility vehicles covered by a bulletin can include most of, if not the entire, production run for one or more model years.

Most service bulletins deal with vehicles manufactured two or three years before a current model year. For instance, most service bulletins issued in 1993 deal with 1990, 1991, and 1992 models. Interestingly, service bulletins are still being issued that apply to models manufactured as long as ten years ago. The repair of one of these may be done for free, or for a shared cost, by the manufacturer if an owner finds out that a bulletin exists.

BREAKING DOWN THE SECRECY BARRIER

Some states are attempting to make it mandatory for auto manufacturers to inform owners directly of inherent defects and repairs. Currently, California, Connecticut, Virginia, and Wisconsin have adopted measures to do just that. Connecticut Public Act No. 90-52 is typical in its wording of the legislation enacted by Virginia, Wisconsin, and California: "A [vehicle] manufacturer shall establish a procedure in this state whereby a consumer (1) shall be informed of any adjustment program applicable to his motor vehicle and (2) shall be entitled to receive a copy of any service bulletin or index thereof upon request."

Some key parts of the Connecticut law, which are duplicated by Virginia, Wisconsin, and California, leave little room for maneuvering by manufacturers to maintain secrecy. For example, the law states that a new car dealer service department would have to disclose the principal terms and conditions of the manufacturer's adjustment (i.e., payment) program to the consumer seeking repairs for a particular condition, "if the dealer has received a service bulletin concerning such adjustment program or otherwise has knowledge of it."

Furthermore, legislation requires that, within 90 days of adoption of an adjustment program, a manufacturer notify (by first-class mail) all consumers eligible under such a program "of the condition of the motor vehicle that is covered."

The Connecticut, Virginia, Wisconsin, and California laws also protect owners who paid to have their cars fixed because their warranties expired before service advisories were issued. If a service advisory is issued after a repair has been paid for by the owner, reimbursement will be made if the owner presents documentation showing that the repair was done. This documentation should state the make, year, model, and identification number of the car; date the repair was made; mileage on the vehicle when the repair was made; description and cost of the repair; and customer's name and address. A claim has to be made in writing to the manufacturer within two years from the date of the repair.

Other states will undoubtedly pass similar measures. Therefore, if you have a problem with a car you bought new, call or write one of your representatives in the state legislature to find out if your state has enacted an anti–secret warranty measure. If so, get a copy of the bill and follow through on its provisions.

WHAT MOST OF US HAVE TO DO

Since most states still don't have anti–secret warranty laws, how can you find out if a problem you're having with your vehicle has been recognized as an inherent defect in a manufacturer's service advisory? For starters, scan the lists in this part of the book. It covers a limited number of service advisories issued by Buick, Cadillac, Chevrolet, Chrysler, Dodge, Eagle, Ford, Honda, Jeep, Lincoln, Mercury, Nissan, Oldsmobile, Plymouth, Pontiac, and Toyota.

If you find one or more applicable secret warranties on the list that addresses your problem, bring the vehicle to a dealer, present the service manager with the TSB number(s), and ask him to check on the provisions to determine if a repair applies to your vehicle. If he confirms that it does, ask him to call the technical or warranty assessment department of the manufacturer to get authorization to fix the problem free under the provisions of the manufacturer's goodwill policy, assuming that new car warranties have expired. Obviously, if basic, bumper-to-bumper power train, body, or emissions system warranties are still in effect, or if you purchased an extended warranty (see Part IV), there should be no opposition on the part of the dealer or manufacturer to making the free repair.

Don't take the dealer's word that you aren't covered by a warranty or goodwill policy if a warranty has expired. The dealer doesn't have the right to make this determination, since the dealer doesn't pay for the repair; the manufacturer does. If the dealer balks, tell him you want to meet with the manufacturer's field representative. Or contact the manufacturer customer service department yourself. Auto manufacturer addresses and phone numbers are listed in the appendix in the back of this book. If you have to, be a pest. It usually pays.

THAT GOODWILL POLICY

Every car manufacturer has a so-called goodwill policy that provides for free or partially free repairs to correct inherent problems after new vehicle warranties have expired. Although information about this policy is kept under wraps, most times a manufacturer lives up to its provisions when a customer presents proof (i.e., knowledge of a service bulletin) that confirms an inherent problem exists for which a repair has been devised.

If you and your car's manufacturer disagree whether a particular problem falls under the intent of a goodwill policy, you can bring the matter before an arbitration panel (see Part IV). As a last resort, you can sue.

IMPORTANCE OF CAREFUL RECORD KEEPING

If you complain about a problem to the service department where you bought your vehicle, while new car warranties are in effect, but are told there isn't a free repair for it (no TSB), ask for documentation. It should show the date you made the complaint, mileage of the car at the time, description of the vehicle (including its identification number), nature of the problem, and a statement to the effect that the vehicle couldn't be repaired. The document should be signed by someone in authority from the dealer service department. With this documentation, you should be able to have the dealer make the repair for free when and if a service bulletin is issued, even if warranties have expired.

GETTING COPIES OF THOSE SECRET WARRANTIES

Suppose you can't find a description of the problem you're having in the list presented in this part of the book. Or suppose you own a vehicle made by a manufacturer other than the ones mentioned, or an older vehicle. Or maybe you want a copy of an applicable service bulletin to prove that a secret warranty exists. You may be able to get help from the Technical Reference Division (TRD), National Highway Traffic Safety Administration, 400 Seventh St., SW, Washington, DC 20590. TRD's files are complete, up-to-date, and computerized as to year, make, and model of the vehicle in question, including specific problems for which service advisories have been issued. In fact, you can order a complete set of secret warranties (TSBs)—on microfiche—applicable to your vehicle. TRD charges a fee for this service.

A FEW WORDS ABOUT THIS BOOK'S LIST OF SECRET WARRANTIES

This part of the book lists problems in the following categories: (1) engine problems, (2) braking problems, (3) transmission and differential problems, and (4) steering problems.

Where a problem applies to vehicles having certain characteristics, such as a particular size engine, that characteristic is given. If your car doesn't fit the description—for example, if it has a manual transmission rather than the automatic transmission listed—the service bulletin doesn't apply. When no characteristic is indicated, the problem and repair apply across the board to all vehicles of that particular model, no matter what equipment it possesses.

With General Motors vehicles, engine designations 3.3 and 3300 or 3.8 and 3800 should be regarded as the same engine. For example, if a designation on the list indicates that a TSB applies to a 3.3 engine but you have been told that your engine is a 3300, ask a dealership service manager to check the TSB anyway. The repair may apply to your car, since the 3.3 and 3300 engines are essentially, although not exactly, the same.

Included in the category of transmission and differential problems are malfunctions affecting four-wheel as well as two-wheel drive systems. Included in the category of steering problems are conditions that show up as abnormal tire wear.

You will find the following abbreviations used throughout the tables in this book:

> A/C = air conditioning
> ABS = antilock braking
> A/T = automatic transmission
> EGR = exhaust gas recirculation
> MAP = manifold absolute pressure
> M/T = manual transmission
> PCV = positive crankcase ventilation

Although only one repair is usually listed per TSB number, the actual secret warranty may offer a number of different repairs leading to the final repair—an engine overhaul, for example. In most cases, only the final repair is mentioned. That doesn't mean this repair has to be performed on your vehicle. Your problem may be corrected by having one of the lesser repairs made. When an advisory contains the statement "analyze and repair according to this service advisory," it means that there are a number of alternatives to be considered by the mechanic in troubleshooting the problem.

BUICK

Year and Model	Problem	TSB Number and Repair
ENGINE PROBLEMS		
1988-93 Electra, Park Ave., LeSabre, Riviera, Reatta, Regal (3800 engine); 1989-93 Century and Skylark (3300 engine);	Hard starting and stalling when decelerating	**93-6E-3;** replace idle air control valve

BUICK *(cont'd)*

Year and Model	Problem	TSB Number and Repair
1991 LeSabre (3800 engine); 1991-93 Park Ave. Ultra (3800 engine and supercharger)		
1988-91 Skylark (2.3 Quad 4 engine)	Coolant leaks into one or more cylinders	**91-POL-2;** replace cylinder head gasket
1989-90 Skylark Century (3300 engine)	Cold engine knocks	**90-6-10;** replace pistons
1989-91 Regal (3.1 engine)	Cold engine knocks at low ambient temperature	**91-POL-3;** replace engine
1990-91 Regal (3.1 engine); 1991 Roadmaster Estate Wagon	Hard starting and starter motor clash	**91-6D-4;** replace starter motor drive unit
1990-91 Skylark (2.5 engine)	Engine pings	**91-6E-23;** replace programmable read-only memory (PROM)
1990-91 Riviera and Reatta; 1991-92 Park Ave.; 1992 LeSabre	Engine occasionally will not crank and start	**92-8-14;** replace starter relay
1990-92 Regal; 1991-92 Park Ave., Riviera, Reatta; 1992 LeSabre (3800 engine)	Cold engine stalls	**92-6E-10;** replace memory and calibration (MEMCAL) unit
1990-93 Regal (3.1 engine)	Cold engine stalls	**93-6E-20;** replace memory and calibration (MEMCAL) unit
1991 Skylark	Surging on deceleration or when driving with cruise control engaged	**91-73T40-5;** replace A/T governor assembly

BUICK (cont'd)

Year and Model	Problem	TSB Number and Repair
1991 Roadmaster	Engine pings	**91-6E-17A;** replace electronic spark control module and programmable read-only memory (PROM)
1991 Roadmaster Estate Wagon; 1992 Roadmaster sedan	Engine idles erratically	**92-6E-2;** replace throttle position sensor
1991-92 Skylark, Century, Regal, Riviera	Hesitation on acceleration or lack of power	**92-6E-29;** replace fuel pump
1991-92 Park Ave.	Engine won't start on occasion because of a dead battery	**92-8-23A;** replace brake transmission shift interlock solenoid
1991-92 Roadmaster (5.7 engine)	Cold engine knocks	**92-6-21;** replace pistons or engine
1991-93 Skylark (3300 engine)	Cold engine stalls	**93-6E-9;** replace programmable read-only memory (PROM)
1992 Skylark (2.3 engine)	Warm engine stalls while idling	**92-6E-18;** repair idle air control wire
1992 Skylark	Hesitation on acceleration or lack of power	**92-6E-17;** replace fuel pump
1992 Roadmaster	Engine pings	**92-6E-11A;** replace programmable read-only memory (PROM)
1992 Skylark	Loss of coolant	**92-6-14A;** replace outlet hose and engine mount lower strut
1992 Skylark (3300 engine)	Engine knocks	**92-6-20;** replace splash shield
1992-93 Park Ave. Ultra (3800 engine)	Cold engine stalls when started	**93-6E-8;** replace programmable read-only memory (PROM)

BUICK *(cont'd)*

Year and Model	Problem	TSB Number and Repair
1992-93 Park Ave., LeSabre (3800 engine)	Engine misfires	**93-6E-13;** identify misfiring cylinder and replace its spark plug and spark plug cable
1992-93 Skylark	Engine won't start, or starts and stalls, or overheats	**93-8-5;** repair damaged wires
1992-93 models with 3300, 3800, and 3800 supercharged engines	Engine knocks	**93-6-12;** replace power steering pump or main bearings
1993 Regal (3800 engine)	Engine runs rough at slow speeds	**93-6E-7;** replace programmable read-only memory (PROM) or electronic control module

BRAKING PROBLEMS

Year and Model	Problem	TSB Number and Repair
1990 Park Ave.; 1990-91 LeSabre; 1990-92 Skylark	Front brakes fail	**92-5-4A;** overhaul calipers
1991-92 Park Ave. and LeSabre	Brake pedal pulsates when brakes are applied	**92-5-11;** replace rear wheel ABS speed sensor
1991-92 Park Ave. and LeSabre	Rear brake shoes freeze to drums in cold weather	**92-5-5;** replace rear brake shoes
1992 Roadmaster sedan	ABS light comes on for no apparent reason	**92-5-6;** reroute front wheel speed sensor wire
1992 Park Ave. and LeSabre	Rear brake noise, low brake pedal, or one rear wheel locks during braking	**92-5-9;** replace rear brake springs
1992 Roadmaster sedan	Clicking from rear when applying brakes	**92-5-12;** replace brake drums
1992 Skylark (2.3 Quad Four engine)	ABS light comes on for no apparent reason	**92-6E-28;** replace crankcase vent heater

BUICK *(cont'd)*

Year and Model	Problem	TSB Number and Repair
1992-93 Skylark	ABS cycles when driving at low speeds, squawking sound when car is braked to a stop, or rear brake linings wear prematurely	**93-5-3;** replace rear brake linings
1993 Century	Brake drag	**93-5-4;** overhaul brake power booster

TRANSMISSION AND DIFFERENTIAL PROBLEMS

1988-90 Electra, Park Ave., Riviera, Regal, Reatta; 1988-91 LeSabre	A/T inoperative in third gear, Drive, or Reverse	**91-7440-5;** overhaul transmission
1988-91 models with A/T	A/T inoperative in Reverse	**91-7440-3;** replace transmission case
1988-90 Electra, Park Ave., Riviera, Reatta; 1988-91 LeSabre; 1988-92 Century and Regal	A/T downshifts harshly from third to second	**92-74T60-8;** replace control valve
1991 Skylark	A/T won't upshift	**91-73T40-5;** replace transmission governor
1991 Roadmaster	A/T inoperative in Reverse in cold weather	**91-74L60-1;** replace reverse clutch piston seal or the input clutch housing
1991 Century, LeSabre, Regal	A/T leaks fluid	**91-74T60-18;** replace transmission case
1991-93 Park Ave. and Riviera; 1992-93 LeSabre; 1993 Regal	A/T leaks fluid	**93-74T60-3;** seal helix seal converter assembly
1991-92 models with A/T	A/T leaks fluid	**92-74T60-6A:** replace side cover and gasket

BUICK *(cont'd)*

Year and Model	Problem	TSB Number and Repair
1991-92 Roadmaster	A/T gets stuck in first gear	92-74L60-2; replace input carrier-to-output shaft retaining ring
1991-92 Roadmaster	A/T inoperative in Reverse	92-74L60-1; overhaul valve body
1991-92 Century, Regal, LeSabre, Park Ave., Riviera, Reatta	A/T experiences delays in shifting after being parked overnight	92-74T60-9; replace input clutch outer piston seal
1992 LeSabre, Park Ave., Riviera	A/T slips in Drive or is inoperative in Drive	92-74T60-7; replace shift solenoids
1992 Roadmaster	A/T upshifts harshly from first to second	92-74L60-9A; overhaul valve body
1992 LeSabre	A/T is inoperative in Reverse, upshifts harshly from first to second, or downshifts harshly from second to first	92-74T60-11; overhaul valve body
1992 models with A/T	A/T shifts erratically or the engine can be started with A/T in second or third gear	92-74T60-10; repair or replace spacer and channel plates
1992-93 Skylark and Century	A/T slips in Reverse or is inoperative in Reverse	93-73T40-2; replace low and reverse clutch return spring and ring
1993 Park Ave., LeSabre, Riviera	A/T torque converter clutch does not engage	93-74T60-5; replace pulse width modulator solenoid

STEERING PROBLEMS

1990-92 Riviera	Car drifts or pulls to side on a level road	92-3-15; set wheel alignment and install transaxle mount kit
1992-93 Skylark	Car drifts or pulls to side on a level road	93-3-8; replace upper strut mount assemblies

BUICK *(cont'd)*

Year and Model	Problem	TSB Number and Repair
1992-93 Roadmaster	Steering wheel is slow to straighten from a turn	93-3-9; replace power steering gear valve assembly and pump actuator

CADILLAC

Year and Model	Problem	TSB Number and Repair

ENGINE PROBLEMS

1988-90 Allante, DeVille, Seville, Fleetwood, Eldorado	Oil leak	90-71; replace oil feed pipe or repair or replace the engine
1988-92 DeVille, Seville, Fleetwood, Eldorado	Engine misses at idle, surges, backfires, loses power, pings, keeps running after ignition is shut off, or occasionally won't start	92-76; repair electric system
1988-92 Allante; 1991-92 DeVille, Seville, Fleetwood, Eldorado	Engine occasionally won't start, is hard to start, hesitates, or loses power	92-58A; repair fuel pump circuit or replace the fuel pump
1989-90 Allante, DeVille, Seville, Fleetwood, Eldorado	Oil leak	90-44; replace oil cooler line seals and oil filter adapter
1989-93 DeVille, Fleetwood, Sixty Special	Engine occasionally hesitates, runs rough, or lacks power	93-123; replace fuel tank
1990 DeVille, Seville, Fleetwood, Eldorado	CHECK ENGINE light glows	92-8; replace air pump or air valve
1990 DeVille and Fleetwood	Engine overheats	91-74; rewire cooling fan

CADILLAC *(cont'd)*

Year and Model	Problem	TSB Number and Repair
1990 DeVille, Seville, Fleetwood, Sixty Special (4.5 engine)	Engine stalls when cold	**90-2A;** replace programmable read-only memory (PROM)
1990 DeVille and Fleetwood	Engine hesitates or misses	**90-46;** reposition fuel pump
1990 Brougham (5.7 engine)	Engine stalls, won't start, or is hard to start	**90-47;** replace fuel pump ground wire screw
1990 DeVille, Seville, Fleetwood, Eldorado	Engine is hard starting on first start of the day	**90-50;** replace fuel pressure regulator
1990 DeVille, Seville, Fleetwood, Eldorado	Engine idles rough, hesitates, or surges	**90-59;** replace EGR vacuum hose
1990 Brougham (5.7 engine)	Cold engine hesitates, surges, or pings	**90-77;** replace programmable read-only memory (PROM)
1990-91 DeVille, Seville, Fleetwood, Eldorado	Cold engine knocks	**92-45;** install piston liners
1990-91 Brougham (5.7 engine)	Engine gives off blue exhaust smoke when started	**92-27;** replace exhaust valve stem seals
1990-92 DeVille, Fleetwood, Sixty Special	Engine hesitates or loses power on turns and sharp curves	**92-116;** replace fuel pump strainer
1990-92 DeVille, Seville, Fleetwood, Eldorado	Engine occasionally idles rough	**92-88;** replace fuel pressure regulator or fuel injectors
1990-92 Brougham	Engine won't start or is hard starting when cold, hesitates, idles rough, or loses power	**92-47;** replace fuel hose

CADILLAC *(cont'd)*

Year and Model	Problem	TSB Number and Repair
1990-92 DeVille, Seville, Fleetwood, Eldorado	Engine occasionally stalls when put into gear, hesitates, or misses	92-9; reposition distributor
1990-92 DeVille, Seville, Fleetwood, Eldorado	Cold engine stalls or hesitates, or stalls when decelerating	93-44; reposition starter ground, or replace throttle position sensor or programmable read-only memory (PROM)
1991 Brougham	SERVICE ENGINE SOON light glows or engine surges when idling, idles rough, or hesitates	91-36; service throttle position sensor
1991 Brougham	Engine hesitates on acceleration	91-42; replace programmable read-only memory (PROM)
1991-92 Brougham	SERVICE ENGINE SOON light glows or engine idles rough	93-15; replace throttle position sensor
1991-92 DeVille, Seville, Fleetwood, Eldorado	SERVICE ENGINE SOON light glows; cruise control may not operate	93-26; repair electric system or replace the Park-Neutral switch
1991-92 Brougham	Engine hesitates, is hard starting, or pings	93-115; replace programmable read-only memory (PROM) or electronic spark control module
1991-92 Brougham (5.7 engine)	Cold engine knocks	93-117; replace engine or pistons
1991-93 all models with 4.5 and 4.9 engines	Engine knocks	93-1; replace main bearings and crankcase
1992 Seville and Eldorado	Oil leak	92-97; replace oil cooler lines

CADILLAC (cont'd)

Year and Model	Problem	TSB Number and Repair
1992 DeVille, Fleetwood, Sixty Special; 1992-93 DeVille, Seville, Eldorado, Sixty Special	Oil leak	**93-82;** replace oil pressure switch
1993 Allante, Seville, Eldorado (4.6 engine)	Engine surges or runs rough	**93-63;** replace control module
1993 Seville and Eldorado	Engine loses power or hesitates	**93-49;** replace fuel sender
1993 Allante, Seville, Eldorado	Engine is hard starting	**93-50;** replace fuel sender
1993 Allante, Seville, Eldorado	Oil leak	**93-39A;** replace oil filter adapter
1993 Allante, Seville, Eldorado	Engine occasionally misses or surges while cruising	**93-101;** reposition ignition system wiring

BRAKING PROBLEMS

1990-91 Brougham	Brake pedal pulsates at slow speeds	**91-26;** replace rear wheel ABS speed sensor
1991-92 DeVille and Fleetwood	Rear brake shoes freeze to brake drums in cold weather	**92-52;** replace brake shoes
1991-92 DeVille, Fleetwood, Sixty Special	Brake pedal pulsates at slow speeds	**92-123;** replace rear wheel ABS speed sensor
1991-92 DeVille and Fleetwood	ABS warning light comes on when trunk lid release switch is pressed	**92-28A;** replace trunk lid release actuator

CADILLAC *(cont'd)*

Year and Model	Problem	TSB Number and Repair
1991-93 DeVille and Fleetwood	ABS warning light comes on occasionally and a code 61 is set in the computer	**93-97;** replace ABS pump relay
1992 DeVille and Fleetwood	Noise from rear brakes	**93-43;** replace rear brake springs

TRANSMISSION AND DIFFERENTIAL PROBLEMS

1990 Brougham	A/T fluid leak	**91-4A;** replace transmission speed sensor
1990-91 Seville and Eldorado	Loss of grease from drive axle boot	**91-22;** replace boot and reposition battery-to-alternator cable
1991 DeVille, Seville, Fleetwood, Eldorado	A/T shifts erratically	**91-62;** replace vehicle speed sensor
1991 DeVille and Fleetwood	Difficulty in shifting out of Park	**91-56;** adjust brake-transaxle shift interlock
1991-92 Allante, DeVille, Seville, Fleetwood, Eldorado	A/T fluid leak	**92-79;** replace side cover
1991-92 DeVille, Seville, Fleetwood, Eldorado	Delayed Drive or Reverse when engine is cold	**92-57;** replace input clutch piston outer seal
1991-93 DeVille, Seville, Fleetwood, Eldorado	A/T fluid leak	**93-42;** replace helix converter seal
1993 Allante, Seville, Eldorado	A/T fluid leak	**93-70;** repair case
1993 Allante, Seville, Eldorado	A/T won't shift out of third in a 3-2 downshift or won't shift out of second in 2-3 upshift	**93-58;** replace lower control valve

CADILLAC *(cont'd)*

Year and Model	Problem	TSB Number and Repair
1993 DeVille and Sixty Special	A/T can't be shifted out of Park in cold weather	**93-C-3;** replace brake/transmission shift interlock solenoid
1993 Allante, Seville, Eldorado (4.6 engine)	A/T shifts harshly	**93-63;** replace power train control module

CHEVROLET

Year and Model	Problem	TSB Number and Repair

ENGINE PROBLEMS

Year and Model	Problem	TSB Number and Repair
1989-90 C&K trucks (4.3 engine and M/T)	Engine idles too fast	**90-320-6E;** replace programmable read-only memory (PROM)
1989-90 Geo Prizm	Engine surges when coasting above 45 mph	**90-443-6E;** replace manifold absolute pressure sensor and wire connector
1989-90 Geo Prizm	Cold engine stalls	**90-157-6E;** replace electronic control module
1989-91 T trucks (4.3 engine)	Oil leak	**91-23-6A;** replace oil filter adapter
1990 Beretta GTZ (2.3 engine)	Engine misses or loses power	**90-244-6E;** repair fuel injection system
1990 Beretta GTZ (2.3 engine)	Engine misses, backfires, idles rough, or is hard to start	**90-385-6D;** replace ignition coils
1990 Beretta GTZ (2.3 engine)	Rattle from engine compartment	**90-317-6A;** replace oil filter
1990 Lumina (2.5 engine and A/T)	Cold engine surges, stalls, or is hard to start	**90-264-6E;** replace memory and calibration (MEMCAL) unit

CHEVROLET *(cont'd)*

Year and Model	Problem	TSB Number and Repair
1990 Lumina (3.1 engine)	Cold engine hesitates or stalls	**90-33-6E;** replace memory and calibration (MEMCAL) unit
1990 Lumina (3.1 engine)	Cold engine knocks at low ambient temperature	**90-445-6A;** replace engine or pistons
1990 Camaro (3.1 engine and A/T)	Cold engine stalls	**90-268-6E;** replace memory and calibration (MEMCAL) unit
1990 Geo Storm (M/T)	Engine surges at 35–55 mph	**90-439-6;** replace EGR valve
1990 light trucks (7.4 engine)	Cold engine idles rough or hesitates	**90-163-6E;** replace programmable read-only memory (PROM)
1990-91 light trucks (4.3 engine)	Oil leak	**91-52-6A;** replace front crankshaft seal
1990-91 Beretta GTZ (2.3 engine)	Loss of coolant or white exhaust smoke	**91-525-6A;** replace cylinder head gasket
1990-91 Cavalier, Beretta, Corsica (2.2 engine and M/T)	Engine surges on deceleration	**91-514-7B;** replace programmable read-only memory (PROM)
1990-91 Beretta and Corsica	Engine overheats	**91-492-6B;** rewire cooling fan
1990-91 Camaro (5.0 or 5.7 engine)	Engine idles rough, misses, surges, or hesitates	**91-105-6;** repair engine wiring
1990-91 Camaro (5.0 engine)	Engine stalls when idling or on deceleration	**91-76-6E;** replace memory and calibration (MEMCAL) unit
1990-91 S&T trucks (4.3 engine and 5-speed M/T)	Engine idles rough or surges on deceleration	**91-516-6E;** replace memory and calibration (MEMCAL) unit

CHEVROLET *(cont'd)*

Year and Model	Problem	TSB Number and Repair
1990-92 Cavalier, Beretta, Corsica (3.1 engine and M/T); 1991-92 Lumina (3.4 engine)	Cold engine stalls	**92-302-6E;** replace memory and calibration (MEMCAL) unit
1990-92 Geo Storm	Engine idling speed is erratic	**92-62-6A;** service throttle body
1990-92 Geo Storm	Cold engine loses power, stalls, or hesitates when accelerated	**92-225-6E;** replace electronic control module
1990-92 Geo Storm	Engine idles rough following deceleration	**92-233-6E;** replace electronic control module
1990-92 Camaro (3.1 engine)	Cold engine stalls or hesitates	**92-191-6E;** replace memory and calibration (MEMCAL) unit
1990-92 Corvette (5.7 engine)	Engine won't start	**92-307-6;** replace starter
1990-93 S-10 truck (2.8 engine and M/T)	Engine pings, surges, or idles too fast when cold	**93-265-6E;** replace programmable read-only memory (PROM)
1991 Caprice (5.0 engine)	Oil in air cleaner housing	**91-28-6;** replace PCV valve
1991 Caprice and Camaro (5.0 engine)	Rattle or click from engine compartment	**91-49-6A;** modify torque converter cover
1991 Caprice and Camaro (5.0 engine)	Engine surges while idling, hesitates at slow speed, idles rough, or displays a glowing SERVICE ENGINE SOON light	**91-60-6E;** replace throttle position sensor
1991 Lumina (3.1 engine)	Engine won't start or is hard to start	**91-506-6C;** replace variable fuel pulse dampener
1991 S&T trucks	Engine won't start	**91-47-6;** replace a terminal of the electronic control module

CHEVROLET *(cont'd)*

Year and Model	Problem	TSB Number and Repair
1991-92 Cavalier and Lumina	Engine loses power, performs sluggishly, or hesitates	**92-176A-6C;** replace fuel pump
1991-92 Cavalier, Beretta, Corsica, Camaro, Lumina, Corvette; 1992 light trucks, vans, and Lumina APV	Cold engine stalls, won't start, hesitates, or loses power	**92-227-6E;** clean fuel system or replace fuel pump
1991-92 Caprice (5.7 engine and A/T)	Cold engine knocks	**92-358A-6;** replace engine or pistons
1991-92 Camaro (5.0 engine)	Engine stalls or hesitates in hot weather	**92-350-6C;** replace fuel pump
1991-92 Camaro	Loss of coolant	**92-77-6B;** replace cylinder head
1991-92 Corvette (A/T)	Engine occasionally won't start	**92-322-6D;** repair Park/Neutral switch wire
1991-92 C&K series trucks (5.7 engine and A/T)	Sluggish engine performance	**92-175A-6E;** replace torque converter and memory and calibration (MEMCAL) unit
1991-92 S&T trucks (4.3 engine and A/T)	Sluggish engine performance	**92-84A-7A;** replace accelerator control cable and pedal assembly
1991-92 S truck (2.5 engine and M/T)	Engine surges	**92-292-6E;** replace EGR valve and memory and calibration (MEMCAL) unit
1991-92 C, K, G, P trucks (4.3, 5.7, or 7.4 engine and A/T)	Sluggish engine performance	**92-236-6E;** replace memory and calibration (MEMCAL) unit
1991-93 Caprice (5.0 or 5.7 engine)	Engine pings or performs poorly at slow speeds	**93-122-6E;** replace programmable read-only memory (PROM)

CHEVROLET *(cont'd)*

Year and Model	Problem	TSB Number and Repair
1991-93 Lumina (3.1 or 3.4 engine with theft alarm)	Starter motor clicks, but occasionally doesn't crank engine	**93-275-6D;** rewire theft alarm
1991-93 light trucks and vans (4.3, 5.7, 7.4 engine)	Cold engine knocks on starting	**93-155-6A;** replace oil filter, install synthetic oil, and secure intake manifold
1992 Caprice (5.7 engine)	Engine pings or surges while idling	**92-93A-6E;** replace programmable read-only memory (PROM)
1992 Caprice (4.3 engine)	SERVICE ENGINE SOON light glows	**92-345-6E;** replace programmable read-only memory (PROM)
1992 Caprice, Beretta, Corsica, C&K trucks, G/L/M vans	Poor fuel economy, missing, or rough running	**92-278-6E;** repair terminals of electronic control module
1992 Caprice, Camaro, or Corvette, light trucks, vans (5.0 and 5.7 engine)	Oil leak	**92-304-6A;** replace camshaft plug
1992 Cavalier (2.2 engine and A/T)	Engine idles rough	**92-94A-6E;** increase idle speed
1992 Cavalier (2.2 engine and A/T)	Engine won't start or starts and stalls	**92-136-7A;** repair engine electric wire harness
1992 Cavalier, Beretta, Corsica (2.2 engine)	Engine hesitates or idles rough	**92-226-6E;** replace intake manifold gasket
1992 Beretta and Corsica (3.1 engine)	Engine surges and SERVICE ENGINE SOON light glows	**92-242-6D;** repair EGR system wire
1992 Beretta and Corsica (3.1 engine)	Engine won't start, surges, stalls, or SERVICE ENGINE SOON light glows	**92-253-6D;** repair engine electric wire harness

CHEVROLET (cont'd)

Year and Model	Problem	TSB Number and Repair
1992 Beretta and Corsica (2.2 engine and A/T)	Engine idles rough	**92-148-6E;** increase idle speed
1992 Beretta and Corsica	Engine coolant leaks from radiator outlet hose	**92-224B-6;** replace hose and engine mount lower strut
1992 M, L, G vans and C, K, S, T trucks (4.3 engine)	Engine pings	**92-285A-6E;** replace programmable read-only memory (PROM)
1992 C&K trucks and G vans (5.0 engine)	Cold engine stalls	**92-351-6E;** replace programmable read-only memory (PROM)
1992 S&T trucks (4.3 engine)	Engine pings	**92-244A-6;** replace engine
1992 Corvette (5.7 engine)	Ticking from engine	**92-301-6A;** resecure exhaust manifold heat shield
1992 Corvette (5.7 engine and M/T)	Sluggish performance	**92-214A-7B;** adjust throttle and cruise control cables
1992 Corvette (5.7 engine and A/T)	Engine backfires at a wide open throttle 1-2 upshift	**92-336-6E;** replace memory and calibration (MEMCAL) unit
1992-93 Lumina (3800 engine)	Engine is hard to start or stalls when decelerating	**93-16A-6E;** replace idle air control motor
1992-93 Cavalier, Beretta, Corsica (2.2 engine and M/T)	Engine stalls or runs rough in cold weather	**93-220-6E;** replace memory and calibration (MEMCAL) unit
1992-93 Lumina APV	Engine knocks	**93-165-6;** install main bearing inserts
1993 M&L vans (4.3 engine)	Engine performs poorly or emits black exhaust smoke; SER-VICE ENGINE SOON light glows	**93-112-6E;** replace exhaust crossover pipe

CHEVROLET (cont'd)

Year and Model	Problem	TSB Number and Repair
1993 M&L vans, S&T trucks (4.3 engine)	Engine knocks or makes ticking sound when idling	**93-246-6;** replace engine

BRAKING PROBLEMS

1990 Geo Tracker	Grinding sound when applying brakes	**90-170-5;** replace rear brake shoes
1990 M, G, L vans	Slap, pop, or clunk when releasing brake pedal	**90-255-5;** refinish brake drums
1990 Lumina APV	Squeal when applying brakes	**90-319-5;** replace front linings
1990-91 Geo Storm	Groan when applying brakes	**91-527-5;** replace front disc pads
1990-91 Geo Storm	Brakes feel hard in cold weather	**91-494-5;** replace brake booster
1990-92 Camaro	Parking brake lever slips as it's being applied	**92-129-5;** replace parking brake hand lever assembly
1990-93 Lumina	Brake noise and reduced brake pad life	**93-137-5;** replace front and rear brake pads
1991 Corvette	ABS motor runs by itself or ABS warning light glows	**91-491A-5;** replace electronic brake control module
1992 Corvette	Brake light glows or brakes drag	**92-71A-5;** set brake pedal clearance
1992 Beretta and Corsica	ABS warning light glows	**92-188-5;** replace speed sensors
1992 Caprice	Click in rear when applying brakes	**92-249A-5;** replace rear brake drums

CHEVROLET (cont'd)

Year and Model	Problem	TSB Number and Repair
1992 Lumina APV	Noise from rear brake, one wheel slides, or brake pedal travel increases	**92-334-5;** replace parking brake adjuster spring
1992-93 Cavalier, Beretta, Corsica	ABS cycles at slow speed, squawk when coming to a stop, or premature brake wear	**93-65-5;** replace rear brake and refinish drums
1992-93 Lumina APV	Rear wheel(s) won't rotate in cold weather	**93-37-5;** replace rear brake shoes
1993 Camaro	Moan when applying brakes	**93-121-5;** replace brake dampers

TRANSMISSION AND DIFFERENTIAL PROBLEMS

1988-90 Celebrity; 1990-91 Lumina (A/T)	Lack of third gear, Drive, or Reverse	**91-87-7A;** overhaul transmission
1988-90 Celebrity; 1990-91 Lumina (A/T)	Slipping in Reverse or lack of Reverse	**91-75-7A;** overhaul transmission
1988-90 Celebrity; 1990-92 Lumina	A/T shifts harshly	**92-130-7A;** overhaul control valve
1988-90 Celebrity; 1988-92 Cavalier, Beretta, Corsica; 1990-92 Lumina	A/T slips in Reverse or lack of Reverse	**92-219-7A;** overhaul reverse clutch housing
1988-92 K trucks	Transfer case leaks fluid	**91-508-7D;** replace vent pipe
1988-92 K trucks	Front axle leaks fluid	**92-202-4D;** replace differential seals
1988-92 C, K, R, V trucks and G vans	Rear axle leaks grease	**92-246-4B;** replace pinion seal

CHEVROLET *(cont'd)*

Year and Model	Problem	TSB Number and Repair
1989-91 Caprice, Camaro, Corvette; 1989-91 C, K, R, V, S, T trucks; 1990 G, L, M vans (A/T)	Lack of Reverse or sluggish shift to Reverse in cold weather	**91-493-7A;** overhaul transmission
1990-91 Geo Tracker (A/T)	Harsh 3-2 downshifts or Neutral to Drive shifts	**91-495-7A;** overhaul transmission
1991 Caprice (5.0 engine and A/T)	Harsh 1-2 upshifts	**91-125-7A;** install 1-2 accumulator valve spring
1991 Lumina (3.4 engine and A/T)	Erratic transmission operation	**91-111-7A;** replace speed sensor
1991 C, K, P, R, V trucks and G vans (6.2 engine and A/T)	Harsh 1-2 upshifts	**91-117-7A;** replace control module
1991-92 Lumina (A/T)	Transmission leaks fluid	**92-110A-7A;** replace side cover
1991-92 Lumina (A/T)	Delayed shift to Drive or Reverse when cold	**92-120A-7A;** replace input clutch seal
1991-92 S&T trucks (4.3 engine and A/T)	Transmission won't downshift	**92-84A-7A;** replace accelerator control cable and pedal
1991-92 G van (A/T)	Growl from transmission	**92-239-7A;** replace programmable read-only memory (PROM)
1991-92 C, K, R, V, P trucks and G vans (A/T)	Lack of Reverse	**92-229-7A;** replace rear band
1991-93 Lumina (A/T)	Transmission leaks fluid	**93-53A-7A;** replace helix seal
1991-93 Lumina (A/T)	Whine with A/T in first, second, or third gear	**93-272-7A;** replace bearing assembly

CHEVROLET *(cont'd)*

Year and Model	Problem	TSB Number and Repair
1991-93 C, K, R, V, P trucks and G vans (A/T)	Squeak or shudder when coasting down or with engine idling and A/T in Park or Neutral	**93-114-7A;** replace torque converter
1991-93 C, K, R, V, P trucks and G vans (A/T)	Transmission won't upshift	**93-147-7A;** replace speed sensor
1992 Camaro (5.0 engine and 5-speed M/T)	Abnormal clutch wear	**92-349-7C;** replace clutch
1992 Caprice, Camaro, Corvette; 1992 C, K, S, T trucks; 1992 G, L, M vans (A/T)	Harsh 1-2 upshifts	**92-318-7A;** replace accumulator valve
1992 Lumina (A/T)	Erratic shifting in second or third gear	**92-197-7A;** repair spacer and channel plates
1992 Lumina (A/T)	Loss of Drive, slipping in Drive, or engine can be started with A/T in fourth gear	**92-123-7A;** replace shift solenoid
1992 C, K, P trucks and G vans (A/T)	Loss of third gear or transmission slips in Reverse	**92-299-7A;** replace direct clutch dished plate
1992 S&T trucks (4.3 engine and A/T)	Shudder, because transmission converter clutch engages too soon	**92-75-7A;** replace programmable read-only memory (PROM)
1992-93 Cavalier, Beretta, Corsica, Lumina (A/T)	Lack of Reverse or transmission slips in Reverse	**93-19-7A;** replace reverse clutch return spring
1993 Camaro (5.7 engine and A/T)	Clunk from A/T when shifting from third to second gear	**93-234-7A;** replace valve body plate

CHEVROLET *(cont'd)*

Year and Model	Problem	TSB Number and Repair
1993 C&P trucks and G vans (A/T)	Transmission leaks fluid	**93-185-7A;** replace case extension
1993 S truck (2.5 or 2.8 engine and 5-speed M/T)	Squawk with M/T in fifth gear and engine cold	**93-274-7B;** install input shaft blocker ring wave spring in transmission

STEERING PROBLEMS

Year and Model	Problem	TSB Number and Repair
1988-92 C&K trucks	Loss of power steering on start-up in cold weather	**92-333-3B;** replace steering gear valve
1991 Caprice	Steering wheel is slow returning to normal position after a turn	**91-81-3B;** replace the steering gear valve
1992-93 Beretta and Corsica	Steering pull	**93-171-3;** replace upper strut mounts
1992-93 Beretta and Corsica (2.2 engine)	Whine when steering wheel is turned	**93-236-3B;** replace power steering pump

CHRYSLER, DODGE, PLYMOUTH, JEEP, AND EAGLE

Year and Model	Problem	TSB Number and Repair

ENGINE PROBLEMS

Year and Model	Problem	TSB Number and Repair
1988-93 Caravan, Voyager, Town & Country; 1989-93 Spirit, Acclaim, LeBaron sedan, Dynasty, New Yorker; 1990-93 Daytona, LeBaron coupe and convertible; 1992-93 Shadow and Sundance (3.0 engine)	Excessive oil loss	**9-18-92A;** replace valve stem seals and cylinder head

CHRYSLER, DODGE, PLYMOUTH, JEEP, AND EAGLE *(cont'd)*

Year and Model	Problem	TSB Number and Repair
1988-91 Premier	Cold engine stalls; warm engine pings or surges	**18-53-91;** replace engine control module
1988-91 Monaco and Premier	Cold engine stalls; warm engine pings or surges	**18-20-92;** replace engine control module
1988-92 Comanche, Cherokee, Wrangler; 1993 Grand Cherokee (4.0 engine)	Loss of engine coolant	**9-11-92;** replace cylinder head
1989-90 Spirit, Acclaim, Dynasty, New Yorker, Daytona, Lancer, LeBaron, Aries, Reliant, Omni, Horizon, Dakota, Shadow, Sundance, Caravan, Voyager (2.2 or 2.5 engine)	Oil leak at cylinder head cover	**9-17-89;** replace cylinder head cover
1989-90 models with 2.2 or 2.5 turbocharged engines	Excessive oil loss (oil present in air cleaner housing)	**9-4-90;** replace cylinder head cover
1989-92 Summit (1.5 engine and A/T)	Engine surges at 45–55 mph	**18-52-90;** replace A/T fluid
1989-90 Summit (1.5 engine)	Cold engine stalls, surges, or hesitates on acceleration	**18-57-91;** replace cylinder head cover
1990 Ram models (5.2 engine)	Hot engine is hard to start	**18-18-89;** replace throttle body
1990 Acclaim, Spirit, LeBaron, Dynasty, New Yorker, Daytona, Caravan, Voyager, Town & Country (3.0 engine)	Ticking sound from engine	**9-2-90;** replace rocker arms

CHRYSLER, DODGE, PLYMOUTH, JEEP, AND EAGLE *(cont'd)*

Year and Model	Problem	TSB Number and Repair
1990 Dynasty, New Yorker, Caravan, Voyager, Town & Country, Imperial	Engine leaks oil	9-3-90; install plugs in crankshaft flange
1990 Caravan and Voyager (3.0 engine)	Engine dies or runs poorly when A/C is on	18-24-90; repair A/C condenser fan wire
1990 Daytona, LeBaron coupe and convertible, Shadow, Sundance (2.2 turbocharged engine)	Engine loses power or CHECK ENGINE light glows during high-speed acceleration	18-36-90; install turbo overboost control components
1990 Acclaim, Spirit, LeBaron (3.0 engine and A/T)	Engine surges when cruising over 45 mph	21-6-90; replace engine control module
1990 Acclaim, Spirit, LeBaron, Dynasty, New Yorker, Daytona, Imperial	Engine stalls immediately upon starting	14-3-91; replace engine control module
1990 Daytona, LeBaron coupe and convertible (3.0 engine and M/T)	Cold engine idles rough or stalls with ambient temperature at 60°–90°F	18-1-92; replace engine control module
1990 Acclaim, Spirit, LeBaron, Dynasty, New Yorker, Daytona, Caravan, Voyager, Town & Country (3.0 engine and A/T)	Cold engine idles rough or stalls with ambient temperature at 60°–90°F	18-21-92; replace engine control module
1990 Ram and Dakota models (3.9, 5.2, or 5.9 engine)	Warm engine runs rough during deceleration	18-26-90; replace engine control module
1990 Comanche, Cherokee, Wagoneer, Wrangler (2.5 engine)	Warm engine idles rough	18-51-90; replace engine control module wiring harness

CHRYSLER, DODGE, PLYMOUTH, JEEP, AND EAGLE *(cont'd)*

Year and Model	Problem	TSB Number and Repair
1990 Talon (2.0 turbocharged engine)	Hot engine won't start	18-55-91; install modulator in engine control module wiring
1990 Talon	Indication of low oil pressure	8-51-90; replace oil pressure gauge
1990 Laser	Indication of low oil pressure	8-3-90; replace oil pressure gauge
1990 Omni and Horizon; 1990-92 Acclaim, Spirit, Daytona, LeBaron coupe and convertible, Dakota, Sundance, Shadow, Caravan, Voyager (2.2 or 2.5 engine and M/T)	Engine idles rough at times after decelerating from a speed	18-7-92A; replace idle air control motor
1990-91 Dynasty, New Yorker, Imperial (3.3 or 3.8 engine)	Cold engine stalls, idles rough, or hesitates	18-5-91; reposition purge solenoid vacuum
1990-91 Monaco	Cold engine pings, stalls, or surges	18-3-91; replace engine control module
1990-91 Dynasty, New Yorker, Caravan, Voyager, Town & Country, Imperial (3.3 or 3.8 engine)	Cold engine idles rough with ambient temperature at 60°–90°F	18-4-91A; replace intake manifold gasket and fuel injectors
1990-91 Dynasty, New Yorker, Caravan, Voyager, Town & Country, Imperial (3.3 engine)	Engine leaks oil	9-6-90A; replace crankshaft and main rod bearings
1990-92 Spirit, Acclaim, Dynasty,	Cold engine is hard to start or loses power	18-4-93; clean throttle body

CHRYSLER, DODGE, PLYMOUTH, JEEP, AND EAGLE *(cont'd)*

Year and Model	Problem	TSB Number and Repair
New Yorker Salon, Daytona, LeBaron, Caravan, Voyager (3.0 engine)	occasionally when decelerating from a slow speed	
1990-92 Talon and Laser (2.0 engine)	Cold engine hesitates or stalls	**18-22-92;** clean valves, cylinder head, and throttle body
1990-92 Acclaim, Spirit, LeBaron, Dynasty, New Yorker Salon, Daytona, Caravan, Voyager, Town & Country; 1992 Sundance and Shadow (3.0 engine)	Engine knocks when warm	**9-2-92;** replace engine control module
1991 Dynasty, New Yorker Salon, Imperial, Fifth Ave.	Engine stalls when started	**14-1-91;** replace engine control module
1991 Spirit, Acclaim, LeBaron, Dynasty, New Yorker, Daytona, Shadow, Sundance, Caravan, Voyager, Town & Country	Engine idles rough or runs poorly at slow speed	**18-2-91;** replace engine control module
1991 Ram trucks (3.9 engine and A/T)	Poor fuel economy	**18-16-91;** replace engine control module
1991 Ram trucks	Engine idles rough and throws off black exhaust	**18-30-90;** replace fuel line
1991 Cherokee and Comanche (4.0 engine)	Engine misses or displays high temperature gauge reading	**18-51-91;** repair wiring
1991-92 Caravan, Voyager, Town & Country	Engine loses power or stalls while driving	**14-6-92;** replace fuel pump module

CHRYSLER, DODGE, PLYMOUTH, JEEP, AND EAGLE *(cont'd)*

Year and Model	Problem	TSB Number and Repair
1991-92 Monaco	Cold engine sags on acceleration just after starting and surges when warmed up while traveling at 30–40 mph with ambient temperature at 60°–90°F	18-12-91; replace engine control module
1991-92 Acclaim, Spirit, LeBaron, Dynasty, New Yorker Salon, Daytona, Caravan, Voyager, Town & Country, Sundance, Shadow (3.0 engine)	Cold engine idles rough or stalls with ambient temperature at 60°–90°F	18-14-92A; replace engine control module
1991-92 Acclaim, Spirit, LeBaron, Dynasty, New Yorker Salon, Daytona, Caravan, Voyager, Ram and Power Ram 50, Laser, Stealth, Colt Vista (1.8, 2.0, 2.4, or 3.0 engine)	Noisy valves	9-6-91; replace tappet lash adjusters
1991-92 Talon; 1992 Summit wagon (1.8, 2.0, or 2.4 engine)	Noisy valves	9-53-9; replace tappet lash adjuster
1991-92 Comanche, Cherokee, Wrangler (4.0 engine)	Engine is hard to start or stalls immediately after starting	18-12-92; replace fuel pump outlet hose
1991-92 Comanche and Cherokee (4.0 engine and A/T)	Cold engine clatters on acceleration	18-10-93; replace power train control module
1991-92 Premier	Cold engine sags on acceleration just after starting and then	18-56-01; replace engine control module

CHRYSLER, DODGE, PLYMOUTH, JEEP, AND EAGLE *(cont'd)*

Year and Model	Problem	TSB Number and Repair
	surges when warm while cruising at 30–40 mph with ambient temperature at 60°–90°F	
1991-92 Premier	Engine loses power	**14-51-92;** replace fuel pump module
1991-93 Ram and Dakota models (3.9, 5.2, 5.9 engine)	Engine occasionally loses power, stalls, or won't start	**14-5-93B;** replace fuel pump module
1992 Acclaim, Spirit, LeBaron, Dynasty, Daytona, Sundance, Shadow, Caravan, Voyager (3.0 engine)	Engine leaks oil	**9-14-92;** replace oil filter bracket gasket
1992 Acclaim, Spirit, Dynasty, Daytona, LeBaron coupe and convertible, Sundance, Shadow, Caravan, Voyager (2.2 or 2.5 engine)	Cold engine is hard to start, idles rough, or hesitates on acceleration in cold weather	**18-13-92A;** replace intake manifold
1992 Dynasty, New Yorker Salon and Fifth Ave., Town & Country, Caravan, Voyager, Imperial (3.3 or 3.8 engine)	Engine pings	**18-17-91;** reset ignition spark advance
1992 Caravan, Voyager, Town & Country (3.0 engine)	CHECK ENGINE light glows	**18-23-92;** replace manifold absolute pressure sensor
1992 Ram and Dakota models (3.9 or 5.2 engine)	Engine leaks oil	**9-7-92;** replace distributor
1992 Ram van and Dakota models (3.9 engine and A/T)	Cold engine hesitates or idles rough	**18-3-93;** replace engine control module

CHRYSLER, DODGE, PLYMOUTH, JEEP, AND EAGLE *(cont'd)*

Year and Model	Problem	TSB Number and Repair
1992 Ram trucks (diesel engine)	Engine surges when cruise control is on	**18-5-92;** replace engine control module
1992 Comanche and Cherokee (4.0 engine)	Engine idles rough when transmission is in gear	**18-2-92;** replace engine mounts
1992 Stealth	Engine won't start	**8-24-92;** repair engine wiring
1992-93 Ram and Dakota models, Grand Cherokee, Grand Wagoneer (3.9, 5.2, or 5.9 engine)	Engine idles rough or stalls	**18-2-93;** replace throttle body
1992-93 Ram and Dakota models; 1993 Grand Cherokee	Engine surges or misfires	**18-16-92A;** reset distributor
1992-93 Ram and Dakota models	Warm engine idles rough or stalls on start-up or deceleration with ambient temperature above 70°F	**18-9-93;** replace idle air control motor
1992 Ram and Dakota models; 1993 Grand Cherokee	Engine won't start or performs poorly	**18-4-92A;** repair engine wiring
1993 Sundance, Shadow, Caravan, Voyager (3.0 engine)	Engine is hard to start or won't start in cool or cold weather	**18-1-93;** repair engine wiring
1993 Spirit, Acclaim, LeBaron, Dynasty, Daytona, Shadow, Sundance, Caravan, Voyager, Town & Country (2.5 engine)	Cold engine knocks or idles rough in cold weather	**9-6-93;** replace engine control module

CHRYSLER, DODGE, PLYMOUTH, JEEP, AND EAGLE *(cont'd)*

Year and Model	Problem	TSB Number and Repair
1993 Concorde, Intrepid, Vision	Warm engine is hard to start	**14-7-92;** replace fuel pump
1993 Concorde, Intrepid, Vision (3.5 engine)	Engine consumes oil and emits excessive exhaust smoke	**9-1-93;** replace makeup air restrictor
1993 Caravan, Voyager, Town & Country	Engine overheats	**8-33-92;** replace cooling fan fusible link and module
1993 Grand Cherokee	Cold engine clatters when started if ambient temperature is below 50°F	**9-13-92;** replace engine control module
1993 Grand Cherokee (4.0 engine and A/T)	Vehicle bucks every so often while cruising	**18-7-93;** replace crankshaft position sensor
1993 Grand Cherokee (4.0 engine)	Oil level light flashes, but oil level is normal	**9-10-92;** replace oil level sensor
1993 Grand Cherokee (5.2 engine)	Oil level light glows with oil level only 1/4 inch below FULL	**9-16-92;** replace oil dipstick
1993 Spirit, Acclaim, LeBaron, Dynasty, New Yorker, Shadow, Sundance, Caravan, Voyager, Town & Country, Imperial; 1994 LHS and New Yorker	Engine stalls when started or lacks power	**14-8-93A;** replace fuel pump
1993 Concorde, Intrepid, Vision; 1994 LIIS and New Yorker (3.5 engine)	Engine won't start at times or performs poorly	**9-12-93;** install timing belt tensioner pivot snubber

CHRYSLER, DODGE, PLYMOUTH, JEEP, AND EAGLE *(cont'd)*

Year and Model	Problem	TSB Number and Repair
BRAKING PROBLEMS		
1989-92 Ram models	Rear brake linings wear out prematurely	**5-4-92A;** replace rear shoes and linings
1990 Dynasty and New Yorker	Brake warning light comes on when brakes are applied, but goes out, ABS pump motor cycles for 1–2 seconds, but no fault codes are stored in computer	**5-3-91;** replace ABS accumulator
1990-91 Dynasty, New Yorker, Imperial	Brake pedal doesn't return to fully released position	**5-10-90;** replace ABS hydraulic unit
1990-91 Talon	Shudder or pulsation in brake pedal or squeal when applying brakes	**5-51-91A;** replace pads, rotors, and hubs
1990-91 Power Ram trucks	Noise from front when applying brakes	**5-5-91;** modify front brake shoes
1990-92 Dynasty, New Yorker, Imperial; 1991-92 Caravan, Voyager, Town & Country	Brake pedal doesn't return to fully released position	**5-8-92A;** replace brake pedal return spring
1991 Cherokee	Brake pedal doesn't return to fully released position	**5-51-92;** replace brake pedal return spring
1991-92 Dakota models	Squeak from front when applying brakes	**5-11-92;** replace front pads
1992 Dynasty, New Yorker, Imperial	ABS warning light glows intermittently or continuously	**5-5-92;** install wire jumper harness in ABS light circuit
1992 Spirit and Daytona	Moan or groan from rear when brakes are applied	**5-10-92;** replace rear pads

CHRYSLER, DODGE, PLYMOUTH, JEEP, AND EAGLE *(cont'd)*

Year and Model	Problem	TSB Number and Repair
1992 Dakota models	Moan or howl from rear when brakes are applied	**5-3-92;** install rear brake dampeners
1993 Spirit, Acclaim, LeBaron sedan, Daytona, Caravan, Voyager, Town & Country, Grand Cherokee, Grand Wagoneer	Grinding from front when brakes are applied	**5-4-93;** replace front discs and pads
1993 Caravan, Voyager, Town & Country	ABS warning light comes on and stays on until ignition switch is turned off	**5-10-93;** replace wheel speed sensors
1993 Dakota models	Moan or howl from rear when brakes are applied	**5-3-93;** install rear brake dampeners
1993 Concorde, Intrepid, Vision	ABS warning light glows	**5-1-93;** repair electrical adaptor

TRANSMISSION AND DIFFERENTIAL PROBLEMS

1989-90 Acclaim, Spirit, LeBaron, Dynasty, New Yorker, Daytona, Caravan, Voyager, Town & Country, Imperial (A/T)	Transmission slips during an upshift from second to third or won't go into third, fourth, or Reverse	**21-9-90A;** overhaul transmission
1989-91 Acclaim, Spirit, LeBaron, Dynasty, New Yorker, Daytona, Caravan, Voyager, Town & Country, Imperial (A/T)	Car shudders when transmission upshifts	**21-22-90;** replace clutch discs
1989-91 Dakota models (4-wheel drive)	4-wheel drive indicator light glows and front axle won't disengage	**21-20-92;** install transfer case filter and replace vacuum switch

CHRYSLER, DODGE, PLYMOUTH, JEEP, AND EAGLE *(cont'd)*

Year and Model	Problem	TSB Number and Repair
1989-92 Acclaim, Spirit, LeBaron, Dynasty, New Yorker, Daytona, Caravan, Voyager, Town & Country, Imperial; 1992 Shadow and Sundance (A/T)	Transmission downshifts harshly from second to first	21-16-92; replace transmission control unit
1991 Stealth (turbocharged and M/T)	Gears grind when shifting	21-8-91; replace clutch
1991 Laser, Colt, Stealth (M/T)	Difficult shifting	21-14-91; replace synchronizer spring
1992 Ram models (M/T)	Transmission jumps out of third gear or is difficult to shift into second gear	21-12-92; replace main shaft bearing retainer plate
1992-93 Dakota and Ram models; 1993 Grand Cherokee and Grand Wagoneer (A/T)	Harsh shifting into Reverse or Drive	21-18-92; replace throttle valve cable return spring

FORD, LINCOLN, AND MERCURY

Year and Model	Problem	TSB Number and Repair

ENGINE PROBLEMS

Year and Model	Problem	TSB Number and Repair
1988-90 Crown Victoria, Mustang, Grand Marquis, Mark VII, Town Car, Bronco, F-series trucks, Econoline (5.0 engine)	Excessive oil consumption	90-1-9; replace valve guide seals and piston rings

FORD, LINCOLN, AND MERCURY *(cont'd)*

Year and Model	Problem	TSB Number and Repair
1988-90 Town Car; 1988-91 Crown Victoria, Mustang, Grand Marquis (5.0 engine)	Engine is hard to start or stalls in cold weather	**91-11-5;** repair PCV system
1988-91 Escort (1.9 engine)	Tapping noise from engine	**90-10-9;** replace valve tappets
1988-90 Mustang, Taurus, Thunderbird, Tempo, Cougar, Sable, Mark VII, Continental, Topaz, Bronco, Bronco II; 1988-91 Crown Victoria, Escort, Grand Marquis, Town Car, F-series light trucks, Econoline, Aerostar; 1988-92 Ranger; 1991 Tracer and Explorer	Engine is hard to start, hesitates on acceleration, stalls, or idles rough	**91-25-7;** clean throttle body and modify idle air bypass system
1988-92 Mustang and Ranger (2.3 engine)	Warbling noise from engine compartment	**92-5-11;** replace crankshaft and camshaft sprockets
1988-90 Taurus, Tempo, Sable, Topaz; 1988-91 Mustang, Mark VII, Bronco, F-series light trucks, Econoline	Engine idles rough or stumbles	**93-11-4;** replace fuel injectors
1988-90 Town Car; 1988-91 Crown Victoria, Mustang, Grand Marquis, Mark VII (5.0 engine)	Engine idles too fast on occasion	**91-10-6;** install new wiring

FORD, LINCOLN, AND MERCURY *(cont'd)*

Year and Model	Problem	TSB Number and Repair
1988-90 Bronco II; 1988-92 Ranger; 1991-92 Explorer (2.9, 3.0, or 4.0 engine)	Internal damage because of water entering engine through air intake system	**91-21-10;** overhaul engine
1988-90 Bronco II; 1988-92 Ranger (2.9 engine)	Oil leak	**93-6-12;** replace rocker cover gaskets
1988-91 Taurus, Tempo, Topaz (2.3 or 2.5 engine)	Oil leak	**91-13-7;** replace oil pan gasket
1988-91 Taurus, Sable, Aerostar; 1990-91 Probe; 1991 Ranger (3.0 engine)	Oil leak	**91-7-8;** replace camshaft core plug
1988-91 Festiva	Engine is hard to start or won't start in cold weather	**91-25-5;** replace oil pan and timing belt
1988-91 Tempo and Topaz (2.3 engine and A/T)	Engine is hard to start in cold weather	**92-15-4;** replace A/T fluid
1988-91 Tempo and Topaz (2.3 engine)	Engine stalls	**93-9-6;** replace idle air control valve, throttle position sensor, or fuel injectors
1988-91 Bronco, F-series light trucks, Econoline (4.9, 5.0, 5.8, or 7.5 engine)	Engine lacks power or won't start	**91-12-11;** analyze and repair catalytic converter and associated components
1988-91 Taurus, Sable, Aerostar; 1990-91 Probe; 1991 Ranger (3.0 engine)	Warm engine knocks intermittently when running at idle	**91-9-8;** replace camshaft thrust plate

FORD, LINCOLN, AND MERCURY *(cont'd)*

Year and Model	Problem	TSB Number and Repair
1988-92 Tempo and Topaz (2.3 engine)	Oil leak	**91-23-6;** replace front damper, front cover and seal, or timing chain and gears
1988-92 Festiva	Engine won't start	**92-22-2;** install 35-amp fusible link
1988-92 Mustang, Taurus, Tempo, Thunderbird, Cougar, Sable, Topaz, Continental, Ranger (2.3 or 3.8 engine)	Cold engine hesitates on acceleration, is hard to start, idles rough, or stalls	**93-12-6;** clean intake valves
1988-93 all models	Engine hesitates, stalls, idles rough, or displays poor fuel economy	**93-14-4;** replace cooling system thermostat
1988-93 Bronco, F-series light trucks, Econoline (5.0 or 5.8 engine)	Engine pings	**93-13-10;** replace distributor
1988-92 F-series light trucks and Econoline (7.5 engine)	Engine lacks power or won't start	**92-22-6;** analyze and repair according to service advisory
1988-92 Bronco, F-series light trucks, Econoline	Engine overheats	**92-15-14;** replace fan clutch
1989-90 Probe (2.2 engine)	Tapping noise from engine	**90-26-8;** replace rocker arms
1989-90 Thunderbird and Cougar (3.8 engine)	Engine is hard to start, stalls, idles rough, or pings	**91-9-5;** replace electronic control processor
1989-90 Taurus SHO (3.0 engine)	Engine is hard to start	**90-21-8;** replace fuel pressure regulator

FORD, LINCOLN, AND MERCURY *(cont'd)*

Year and Model	Problem	TSB Number and Repair
1989-90 Taurus SHO	Cold engine hesitates on acceleration or idles rough	**90-21-9;** replace electronic control processor
1989-90 Aerostar (3.0 or 4.0 engine)	Coolant overflows from coolant tank in hot weather	**90-25-15;** install larger capacity tank
1989-90 F-series light trucks and Econoline (7.5 engine)	Oil leak	**89-24-12;** replace oil pan gasket
1989-91 Probe	Engine won't start	**91-16-6;** repair wire connectors
1989-91 Probe	Rough idle	**91-11-3;** replace radiator and engine mounts
1989-90 Taurus SHO (3.0 engine and M/T)	Engine loses power	**91-23-4;** replace clutch
1989-92 Tempo and Topaz (2.3 engine)	Oil leak	**92-3-3;** replace front cover gasket
1989-92 Taurus (3.0 engine)	Engine surges at 55 mph and above	**92-5-6;** replace idle air bypass valve
1989-92 Probe; 1991-92 Escort (1.8 or 2.2 engine)	Engine is hard to start, idles rough, hesitates, or stumbles	**92-7-5;** replace inlet air tube
1989-93 Taurus, Thunderbird, Cougar, Sable, Continental (3.8 engine)	Squeak, chirp, or knock from engine	**92-13-10;** replace rocker arms
1990 Taurus and Sable (3.0 or 3.8 engine)	Engine hesitates or misses on acceleration, or idles rough, stalls, misses, or won't start	**90-10-4;** install wire and resistor

FORD, LINCOLN, AND MERCURY (cont'd)

Year and Model	Problem	TSB Number and Repair
1990 Town Car	Engine won't start on occasion	**90-16-2;** replace neutral-start switch and install deflector around A/T vent
1990 Thunderbird	Engine won't start on occasion	**90-16-3;** replace antitheft module
1990 Probe, Taurus, Sable, Aerostar (3.0 engine)	Oil leak	**90-16-4;** install oil filter mounting insert
1990 Econoline (4.9 engine)	Engine pings	**90-21-12;** replace electronic control processor
1990 Bronco, F-series light trucks, Econoline	Poor performance	**91-14-9;** install MAP sensor connector
1990 Bronco and F-series light trucks (4.9 engine and M/T)	Engine stalls or misses during deceleration	**91-22-8;** replace electronic control processor
1990 Bronco, F-series light trucks, Econoline (5.0 engine and A/T)	Engine surges at slow speed or rolls while idling	**91-2-13;** replace electronic control processor
1990 Bronco, F-series light trucks, Econoline (4.9 engine)	Engine stalls or misses when put into gear	**92-12-17;** replace electronic control processor
1990-91 Probe (3.0 engine and A/T)	Engine idles too fast	**93-3-6;** replace power train control module
1990-91 Ranger (2.3 engine)	Malfunction indicator light goes on (no fault recorded)	**91-20-11;** replace electronic control processor
1990-91 Ranger and Explorer (4.0 engine)	Engine is hard to start or idles rough	**91-17-9;** install wire terminal
1990-91 Ranger and Explorer (4.0 engine)	Cold engine is hard to start or won't start	**91-13-9;** replace ignition switch

FORD, LINCOLN, AND MERCURY *(cont'd)*

Year and Model	Problem	TSB Number and Repair
1990-92 Probe (3.0 engine)	Rough idle	**91-22-4;** replace thermostat
1990-92 Capri	Loss of coolant	**91-25-11;** replace radiator hose clamps
1990-92 F-150 light trucks (4.9 engine and M/T)	Cold engine stalls when started	**92-18-11;** replace electronic control processor
1990-92 Aerostar and Ranger; 1991-92 Explorer (4.0 engine)	Engine knocks	**93-5-11;** replace fuel line
1990-92 Aerostar and Ranger; 1991-92 Explorer (4.0 engine)	Oil leak	**92-14-13;** replace rocker cover gaskets
1990-92 Aerostar and Ranger; 1991-92 Explorer (4.0 engine)	Oil leak	**93-5-12;** replace rear seal
1990-93 Bronco, F-series light trucks, Econoline (4.9 engine)	Engine stalls when started	**93-9-15;** install vacuum switch
1990-93 Bronco and F-series light trucks (4.9 engine)	Knock from engine compartment when accelerating at low speeds	**93-11-8;** replace accelerator cable, A/C, and power steering brackets
1991 Capri	Engine won't start because battery keeps discharging	**90-19-11;** repair luggage compartment light circuit
1991 Town Car (4.6 engine)	Rough idle	**91-11-6;** replace crankcase connector
1991 Thunderbird and Cougar (3.8 or 5.0 engine)	Engine stalls, idles rough, misses, or lacks power	**91-14-4;** replace exhaust gas oxygen sensors

FORD, LINCOLN, AND MERCURY (cont'd)

Year and Model	Problem	TSB Number and Repair
1991 Capri	Loss of coolant	**91-20-7;** replace radiator hoses
1991 Capri (1.6 engine)	Engine makes rattling sound when started in hot weather	**91-7-7;** replace valve adjusters
1991 Capri (1.6 engine)	Engine is hard to start	**91-18-5;** modify battery positive cable
1991 Taurus and Sable (3.0 engine and A/T)	Engine loses power when cruise control is activated	**91-20-4;** replace accelerator cable
1991 Thunderbird and Cougar (3.8 or 5.0 engine)	Engine stalls or stumbles and may not restart	**92-9-2;** replace thick film ignition module
1991 Escort and Tracer (1.8 engine)	Engine malfunction indicator light comes on in cold weather	**92-14-4;** replace electronic control processor
1991 Ranger and Explorer (4.0 engine)	Engine overheats	**91-8-23;** replace fan and fan clutch
1991 Town Car; 1992 Crown Victoria and Grand Marquis	Engine pings or fails state emissions test	**93-5-6;** replace power train control module
1991-92 Capri	Alternator drive belt continually fails	**92-6-10;** replace alternator pulley
1991-92 Capri (1.6 engine)	Engine overheats	**92-7-7;** install 25-amp fuse
1991-92 Mustang (2.3 engine)	Oil leak	**93-17-6;** replace oil pan and gasket
1991-92 Escort and Tracer (1.9 engine)	Engine hesitates or stalls in cold weather	**93-3-5;** replace PCV valve
1991-92 Escort and Tracer (1.8 engine)	Engine knocks	**92-18-5;** replace camshafts

FORD, LINCOLN, AND MERCURY *(cont'd)*

Year and Model	Problem	TSB Number and Repair
1991-92 Bronco, F-series light trucks, Econoline; 1992-93 Escort, Taurus, Sable, Tracer, Continental (1.9, 3.8, or 5.8 engine)	Engine idles too fast after highway cruising	93-9-5; replace idle air control valve
1991-92 Bronco, F-series light trucks, Econoline (4.9 engine)	Engine stalls or misses	92-9-13; replace electronic control processor
1992 Econoline (5.0 engine)	Engine hesitates on acceleration	92-13-15; replace electronic control processor
1991-92 Explorer (4.0 engine)	Engine is hard starting, or stalls or idles rough when started	93-3-15; replace electronic control processor
1991-93 Escort and Tracer (1.9 engine)	Engine pings	92-26-3; remove octane adjust bar
1991-93 Escort, Capri, Tracer (1.6 or 1.8 engine)	Ticking sound from engine	92-17-6; replace valve lifters
1991-93 Town Car; 1992-93 Grand Marquis (4.6 engine)	Engine pings or makes ticking sound	93-17-4; replace radio frequency interference cable
1992 Taurus and Sable (3.0 engine)	Cold engine hesitates or stalls on acceleration	92-19-4; replace electronic control processor
1992 Taurus, Sable, Continental	Engine stalls when coming to a stop	93-14-5; replace converter clutch control solenoid
1992 Econoline (4.9 engine)	Engine won't start	92-20-10; replace wire terminals
1992 Bronco (5.0 engine)	Engine surges when cruising at speeds below 35 mph	93-7-7; replace electronic control processor

FORD, LINCOLN, AND MERCURY *(cont'd)*

Year and Model	Problem	TSB Number and Repair
1992 Ranger (3.0 engine)	Cold engine hesitates when accelerated	**92-14-9;** replace electronic control processor
1992 Ranger (2.3 engine)	Engine pings when idling in hot weather	**93-4-7;** replace electronic control processor
1992 Ranger (3.0 engine)	CHECK ENGINE light glows for no apparent reason	**93-16-12;** replace power train control module
1992 Ranger (2.3 engine)	Engine is hard to start, idles rough, or stalls in hot weather	**93-4-8;** replace electronic control processor
1992-93 Taurus (3.0 engine and M/T)	Engine won't start or is hard to start on occasion	**93-3-8;** replace starter
1992-93 Taurus and Sable (3.0 or 3.8 engine)	Engine won't start	**93-13-5;** repair and insulate engine wire
1992-93 Taurus, Tempo, Sable, Topaz, Ranger, Aerostar (3.0 engine)	Engine cuts out and won't restart	**93-18-5;** replace distributor and camshaft
1992-93 Bronco and F-series light trucks (5.8 engine)	Knock from engine compartment	**93-13-9;** replace fuel line
1992-93 Bronco and F-series light trucks (4.9 engine)	Knock from engine compartment	**93-1-16;** replace fuel line
1992-93 Bronco and F150 light trucks (5.0 engine and A/T)	CHECK ENGINE light glows for no apparent reason	**93-16-11;** replace power train control module
1992-93 Explorer (4.0 engine)	Engine won't start	**93-16-10;** replace battery and cables, and install battery cover
1993 Mark VIII	Engine won't start or is hard to start	**93-18-6;** replace throttle position sensor and install water shield

FORD, LINCOLN, AND MERCURY *(cont'd)*

Year and Model	Problem	TSB Number and Repair
1993 Mark VIII (4.6 engine)	Engine lacks power	**93-10-3;** replace power train control module
1993 Mark VIII	Engine overheats	**93-10-2;** fill cooling system and purge air
1993 Mark VIII (4.6 engine)	Engine won't start in cold weather	**93-7-4;** replace starter
1993 Villager	Engine won't start because battery discharges	**93-18-11;** replace liftgate latch

BRAKING PROBLEMS

Year and Model	Problem	TSB Number and Repair
1988-90 Bronco II; 1988-92 Aerostar, Bronco, Ranger, F-series light trucks, Econoline; 1991-92 Explorer	Brakes grab or bind	**93-11-7;** replace caliper pins
1988-91 Festiva	Rear brake linings wear prematurely and parking brake is hard to release	**92-6-7;** overhaul rear brake mechanism
1988-92 Tempo and Topaz	Squeal or groan when brakes are applied or premature rear brake lining wear	**93-8-6;** replace front or rear pads or linings
1988-92 Continental	Vibration when brakes are applied	**93-9-3;** replace front pads and rotors
1988-92 Aerostar	Rear brakes grab or squeal on first stop of the day in cool, damp weather	**92-21-9;** replace rear linings
1988-93 Bronco and F150	Rear brakes grab or squeal on first stop of the day in cool, damp weather	**93-4-6;** replace rear linings

FORD, LINCOLN, AND MERCURY *(cont'd)*

Year and Model	Problem	TSB Number and Repair
1989-91 F250, F350, E250, E350	Brake pedal fades when truck is loaded or when going down steep grade	**91-20-8**; replace caliper pistons
1989-92 Thunderbird and Cougar	Roughness or pulsation when applying brakes	**92-4-3**; replace front pads and rotors
1989-93 Thunderbird and Cougar	Roughness in pedal when applying brakes	**93-6-3**; replace rear drums
1989-90 Bronco II; 1989-92 Aerostar and Ranger; 1991-92 Explorer	Vibration or noise when applying brakes	**92-14-7**; overhaul calipers, replace linings, or install new steering knuckles or spindles
1990-91 Probe LX and GT	Occasional squeal when applying brakes	**91-3-4**; replace rear pads
1990-91 Aerostar (4-wheel drive)	Vibration or pulsation	**92-4-14**; replace constant velocity halfshaft and left and right axle shafts
1990-92 Crown Victoria, Grand Marquis, Town Car	Trouble engaging parking brake	**93-14-3**; replace vacuum switch
1990-93 Crown Victoria, Grand Marquis, Town Car	Roughness when applying brakes because of premature front rotor failure	**93-16-2**; replace front linings and rotors
1991 Explorer	Snapping or popping from under vehicle	**92-1-6**; replace frame crossmember rivet
1991-92 Escort and Tracer	Squeal from rear when applying brakes	**92-2-2**; replace rear linings
1991-92 Taurus, Sable, Continental, Town Car; 1992 Crown Victoria and Grand Marquis	Brake pedal is slow to return to full extension or doesn't return	**92-19-2**; replace ABS booster

FORD, LINCOLN, AND MERCURY *(cont'd)*

Year and Model	Problem	TSB Number and Repair
1991-93 Escort and Tracer	Excessive effort needed to apply brakes on first few stops of the day	**93-1-7;** replace linings
1991-93 Town Car; 1992-93 Crown Victoria and Grand Marquis	Rear brake linings wear out prematurely	**93-18-3;** replace linings and install rear brake shields
1992 Crown Victoria and Grand Marquis (automatic overdrive)	ABS light glows for no apparent reason	**93-3-3;** replace electronic control unit and repair wire connectors
1992-93 Crown Victoria and Grand Marquis	ABS light glows constantly or intermittently for no apparent reason	**93-10-1;** repair ABS wiring
1992-93 F250, F350, E250, E350	Vibration or shudder when applying brakes	**93-12-14;** replace wheels

TRANSMISSION AND DIFFERENTIAL PROBLEMS

1988-90 Bronco II; 1988-91 Aerostar, Bronco, F150, F250, Ranger; 1991 Explorer (5-speed M/T)	Hard shifting into Reverse or fifth gear	**91-10-15;** replace synchronizer sleeve
1988-91 Aerostar, Bronco, F-series light trucks, Ranger; 1989-90 Bronco II; 1991 Explorer (M/T)	Transmission fluid leak	**91-18-14;** replace clutch slave cylinder
1988-90 Bronco II; 1988-91 Aerostar, F150, Bronco, Ranger; 1991 Explorer (M/T)	Occasional grind or crunch when shifting from second to third gear	**91-18-11;** replace synchronizer

FORD, LINCOLN, AND MERCURY *(cont'd)*

Year and Model	Problem	TSB Number and Repair
1988-90 Continental (A/T)	Harsh 3-2 downshifts	**93-14-13;** replace throttle valve cable or transmission mounts
1988-90 Bronco and F-series light trucks (M/T)	Clutch pedal doesn't fully release and loss of transmission fluid	**90-16-7;** analyze and repair according to service advisory
1988-90 Bronco II; 1988-91 Ranger (M/T)	Vibration or growl when depressing clutch pedal	**91-12-12;** replace hydraulic line
1988-90 F250 and F350	Transmission fluid leak	**90-5-9;** replace output flange nut
1988-91 Taurus, Sable, Continental (A/T)	Erratic shifting	**91-5-7;** replace forward clutch piston
1988-91 F-series light trucks (M/T)	Clutch pedal is hard to depress	**92-2-8;** replace clutch release bearing
1988-92 Taurus, Sable, Continental (A/T)	Erratic shifting or A/T shifts into Neutral by itself when car is brought to a stop	**93-9-11;** replace forward clutch piston
1988-93 Ranger (M/T)	Rattle, scrape, click, or popping sound from clutch	**93-12-18;** replace clutch disc, cover, and plate
1989-90 Taurus SHO (5-speed M/T)	Clutch slips	**91-23-4;** replace clutch
1989-90 Probe (A/T)	Delayed 2-3 upshifts	**90-16-6;** replace oil pump and spool valve
1989-90 Probe (A/T)	No 3-4 upshifts or 2-1 downshifts	**90-4-8;** replace pulse signal generator
1989-90 Crown Victoria, Mustang, Thunderbird, Cougar, Grand	Delayed 3-4 upshifts or 4-3 downshifts	**91-16-12;** overhaul automatic overdrive

FORD, LINCOLN, AND MERCURY (cont'd)

Year and Model	Problem	TSB Number and Repair
Marquis, Mark VII, Town Car, Bronco, F150, E150, E250 (A/T)		
1989-90 Crown Victoria, Mustang, Thunderbird, Cougar, Grand Marquis, Mark VII, Town Car, F150, E150 (A/T)	Harsh, abrupt shifts	91-11-4; analyze and repair according to service advisory
1989-90 Crown Victoria, Grand Marquis, Town Car (A/T)	Loss of overdrive or delayed 3-4 upshifts	90-2-7; analyze and repair according to service advisory
1989-90 Bronco II	Driveline vibration	90-19-4; reinforce rear springs
1989-90 Bronco, F-series light trucks, Econoline (A/T)	Harsh, abrupt 3-4 up-shifts	90-17-11; repair clutch return spring
1989-90 Bronco II and Ranger; 1991 Explorer (4-wheel drive)	Transfer case shifts from 2-wheel to 4-wheel drive by itself	91-18-13; replace control module, electric motor, and wiring
1989-90 Bronco II; 1989-93 Ranger; 1991-93 Explorer; 1992-93 Aerostar, Bronco, F-series light trucks, Econoline (A/T)	Shift quadrant (PRNDL) doesn't show gear that the A/T is in	93-5-14; replace locking tab
1989-91 Econoline and F-series light trucks (A/T)	Transmission has trouble shifting or doesn't shift in cold weather	90-25-17; repair heating system
1989-92 Bronco, F-series light trucks, Econoline (A/T)	A/T overheats and fails	93-12-20; overhaul transmission to improve durability

FORD, LINCOLN, AND MERCURY *(cont'd)*

Year and Model	Problem	TSB Number and Repair
1989-93 Bronco, F-series light trucks, Econoline (A/T)	Metallic ringing sound when shifting from Reverse to Drive	93-12-16; service splines of Park gear and output shaft with special compound
1990 Town Car (A/T)	Transmission fluid leak	90-16-2; replace neutral start switch
1990 Crown Victoria, Mustang, Thunderbird, Cougar, Grand Marquis, Mark VII, Town Car, Bronco, F150, F250, E150 (A/T)	Delayed or no shifting	91-3-9; analyze and repair according to service advisory
1990 Aerostar and Ranger (A/T)	Delayed or no shifting	90-22-17; overhaul transmission
1990 Bronco II	Driveline vibration	90-25-16; overhaul transmission extension housing
1990 Bronco II; 1990-91 Ranger; 1991 Explorer (A/T and 4-wheel drive)	Lack of coupling or delayed engagement of front wheels when shifting into 4-wheel drive	91-18-12; replace clutch coil, lockup collar, front locking hub, and return and sleeve springs
1990-91 Bronco, F-series light trucks, Econoline (A/T)	Initial forward engagement takes 5–20 seconds to occur when A/T is cold	91-25-19; overhaul transmission
1990-91 Ranger; 1991 Explorer (4-wheel drive)	Transfer case won't disengage from 4-wheel drive	91-20-17; replace transfer case return and sleeve springs, and lockup fork
1990-91 Aerostar (A/T)	Transmission fluid leak	92-11-14; replace transfer case seal
1990-93 Aerostar, Ranger, Explorer (A/T)	Harsh 2-3 upshifts	93-16-15; replace backout spring

FORD, LINCOLN, AND MERCURY *(cont'd)*

Year and Model	Problem	TSB Number and Repair
1990-92 Aerostar and Ranger; 1991-92 Explorer (4.0 engine and A/T)	Increase in engine speed when upshifting from second to third	**93-14-21;** replace backout spring
1991 Escort and Tracer (1.9 engine and A/T)	Harsh, abrupt upshifting	**91-1-10;** replace servo return spring
1991 Escort and Tracer	Difficulty shifting gears	**92-2-7;** replace differential
1991 Taurus, Sable, Continental (A/T)	Lack of second gear, delayed 1-2 upshifts, or delayed 3-2 downshifts	**92-19-5;** install main control separator
1991 Taurus, Sable, Continental (A/T)	Delayed shifting or A/T shifts into Neutral during 3-2 downshifts	**91-19-8;** replace control valve retainer
1991 Capri (1.6 engine and A/T)	Delayed or harsh shifting	**91-25-6;** adjust throttle valve cable
1991 Capri	Shift lever separates from housing	**91-1-11;** replace shift lever
1991-93 Escort and Tracer (A/T)	Transmission fluid leak	**93-11-6;** replace torque converter
1992 Taurus (M/T)	Gears clash when shifting	**93-1-12;** replace clutch pressure plate
1992 Tempo and Topaz (3.0 engine and A/T)	Harsh or delayed shifting	**92-3-4;** reposition heater hose and throttle valve cable
1992 Bronco and F-series light trucks (A/T)	A/T shifts too soon or hunts for third or fourth gear	**92-22-5;** replace transmission control switch wiring
1993 Probe (2.0 engine A/T)	Harsh 3-2 downshifts at 40–55 mph	**92-24-9;** replace power train control module

FORD, LINCOLN, AND MERCURY (cont'd)

Year and Model	Problem	TSB Number and Repair
1993 Crown Victoria, Grand Marquis, Town Car (A/T)	Unusually active shifting between gears	93-12-11; replace power train control module
1993 Crown Victoria, Grand Marquis, Town Car, Mark VIII (A/T)	Harsh shifting	93-16-6; replace manual lever position sensor
1993 Taurus, Sable, Continental (A/T)	Shift lever indicator doesn't display gear position	93-16-4; replace shifter bezel
1993 Taurus (3.2 engine and A/T)	Delay in downshifting followed by a harsh bump	93-14-14; replace power train control module
1993 Villager (A/T)	Harsh upshifting when accelerating	93-11-10; replace shift solenoid

STEERING PROBLEMS

1988-90 Bronco II; 1988-92 Bronco, F-series light trucks, Econoline, Ranger; 1991-92 Explorer	Fluid leak from power steering gear	93-6-7; replace steering gear input shaft seal
1988-91 Probe	Car drifts to side while driving at highway speed on a level road	91-24-6; replace strut mounts
1988-92 Continental; 1990-92 Taurus and Sable	Effort needed to steer car on turns	93-1-4; replace power steering gear
1988-92 Bronco, F150, F250	Vehicle pulls to left when brakes are applied	92-18-10; replace radius arm bushing
1988-92 Mark VII; 1988-93 Mustang, Taurus, Tempo, Thunderbird, Sable,	Vehicle wanders or front tires wear prematurely	93-13-2; analyze and repair according to service advisory

FORD, LINCOLN, AND MERCURY *(cont'd)*

Year and Model	Problem	TSB Number and Repair
Topaz, Cougar, Continental, Aerostar; 1991-93 Escort and Tracer; 1993 Mark VIII		
1989-92 Thunderbird and Cougar	Steering wheel vibrates when brakes are applied	**92-4-3;** replace brake shoes and rotors
1990-91 Crown Victoria, Taurus, Grand Marquis, Mark VII, Sable, Town Car; 1991 Continental	Click from steering column when turning wheel	**92-12-3;** replace steering wheel bearings
1991 Explorer	Vehicle drifts or pulls to side	**91-10-12;** adjust caster
1991 Explorer	Vehicle bounces excessively	**90-25-14;** replace shock absorbers
1991-92 Escort and Tracer	Scrape from steering column as wheel is turned	**92-6-8;** repair steering column shroud
1991-92 Town Car; 1992 Crown Victoria and Grand Marquis	Pulsation or vibration in steering wheel at about 45 mph on slight turns	**92-8-6;** replace rear air suspension/electronic variable orifice module
1991-93 Town Car; 1992-93 Grand Marquis	Noise from steering column when accelerating	**93-5-4;** service steering shaft

HONDA

Year and Model	Problem	TSB Number and Repair

ENGINE PROBLEMS

1988-92 Civic; 1990-92 Accord;	Hard starting, pinging, and poor performance	**89-27;** replace distributor, top dead center sensor, crank

HONDA (cont'd)

Year and Model	Problem	TSB Number and Repair
1992 Prelude	traceable to ignition system	angle sensor, and cylinder sensor
1989-91 Civic	Oil leak around spark plugs	**91-16;** replace camshaft holders
1989-91 Civic	Engine occasionally idles rough	**91-31;** repair throttle angle sensor
1990 Accord	Engine won't start	**93-32;** replace distributor
1990-91 Accord	Oil leak around timing belt cover	**91-35;** replace camshaft oil seal
1992 Civic, Accord, Prelude	Oil leak around oil pressure switch	**92-3;** replace oil pressure switch
1992 Civic	Engine is hard to start	**92-43;** replace fuel pump

BRAKING PROBLEMS

Year and Model	Problem	TSB Number and Repair
1988-90 Prelude	Front brake pads wear out prematurely or squeak	**89-38;** replace pads
1988-91 Prelude	Rear brake pads wear out prematurely or squeak	**91-27;** replace pads
1990-91 Prelude; 1991 Accord SE	ABS warning light glows	**90-38;** replace ABS modulator
1992 Accord EX	Brake fluid leaks from ABS pump	**92-25;** replace ABS pump inlet hose fitting

TRANSMISSION AND DIFFERENTIAL PROBLEMS

Year and Model	Problem	TSB Number and Repair
1990 Accord (A/T)	Delayed engagement of first gear when accelerating	**89-40;** adjust A/T throttle pressure control cable
1990 Accord (M/T)	Difficulty shifting gears	**90-36;** replace shift lever assembly and cables
1990 Accord (A/T)	Transmission gets stuck in third or fourth gear	**90-39;** replace A/T control unit

HONDA *(cont'd)*

Year and Model	Problem	TSB Number and Repair
1990-91 Accord	Grease leaks from driveshaft constant velocity (CV)	**92-10;** repair CV joint boots

STEERING PROBLEMS

Year and Model	Problem	TSB Number and Repair
1989-91 Civic	Abnormal front tire wear	**90-30;** adjust toe angle to new specs
1990-93 Accord	Abnormal front or rear tire wear	**93-11;** replace tires and adjust toe and caster angles to new specs
1992 Accord	Car drifts to left when driving at highway speeds	**92-23;** adjust rear beam
1992-93 Prelude	Car drifts to right	**93-16;** replace power steering spool valve
1992-93 Civic	Premature tire wear	**93-29;** rotate tires and reset front toe

NISSAN

Year and Model	Problem	TSB Number and Repair

ENGINE PROBLEMS

Year and Model	Problem	TSB Number and Repair
1989-90 240SX	Idling speed fluctuates when engine is warm	**91-22;** replace electronic control processor
1989-90 240SX	Oil leak	**90-103;** replace oil pressure switch
1989-90 Maxima	Idling speed fluctuates	**90-73;** replace air cleaner
1990 300ZX	Oil leak or squeal from engine	**91-27;** replace belt tensioner
1990 300ZX	Engine pings	**91-40;** replace PCV valve

NISSAN *(cont'd)*

Year and Model	Problem	TSB Number and Repair
1990 300ZX (non-turbocharged)	Engine pings	**90-97;** replace electronic control processor
1990 300ZX	Engine pings	**92-14;** replace camshaft, cylinder head, and crank angle sensor
1990 D21 light trucks	Oil leak	**91-38;** replace crankshaft rear oil seal
1990 light trucks (2-wheel drive)	Starter motor grinds as engine is started	**90-75;** adjust inhibitor switch and manual control linkage
1990-91 300ZX	Engine idles rough	**93-105;** replace intake valves
1990-91 300ZX	Engine makes tapping sound	**92-16;** replace automatic tensioner
1990-92 light trucks (2-wheel drive)	Idling speed fluctuates	**92-52;** repair sensor wiring
1991 Sentra	Valve noise and poor engine performance because of camshaft wear	**92-4;** replace camshaft
1991-93 Sentra	Engine hesitates, loses power, or expels black exhaust	**93-118;** repair mass air flow sensor wire
1991-93 Sentra	Engine won't start, stalls, hesitates on acceleration, or lacks power	**93-79;** replace fuel pump
1992 Maxima (M/T)	Engine knocks	**92-20;** remove ingested power valve from inside engine screw and repair damage
1992-93 Maxima	Engine lacks power on acceleration	**93-116;** repair electronic fuel injection wire harness or replace control module
1993 Altima	Rough idling	**93-117;** adjust idle speed

NISSAN *(cont'd)*

Year and Model	Problem	TSB Number and Repair
BRAKING PROBLEMS		
1989-92 Maxima	Brakes squeak or squeal	**93-2;** replace pads
1990 240SX	Brakes squeak or squeal	**90-56;** replace pads
1990 300ZX	Brakes clunk when car is backing up	**89-163;** replace pad pins
1991-92 Sentra	Noise when applying brakes	**92-50;** replace pads
1992 Maxima GXE	Squeal from rear when brakes are applied	**93-42A;** replace rear brake backings

TRANSMISSION AND DIFFERENTIAL PROBLEMS		
1988-90 Sentra and NX (M/T)	Transmission fluid leak	**90-24;** replace transmission case bolts
1988-90 Sentra and NX (A/T)	Transmission fluid leak	**90-10;** replace transmission cover bolts
1988-92 240SX and Pathfinder (M/T)	Clutch slips or vibrates	**92-9;** replace clutch
1988-92 Pathfinder and light trucks (M/T)	Gear shift vibrates when accelerating in third gear	**93-21A;** replace third gear
1989-90 Maxima (A/T)	A/T shifts erratically	**90-9;** overhaul A/T
1989-90 Maxima; 1990 Stanza (A/T)	Delayed downshifts, or engine can be started with A/T in D4	**90-81;** replace valve body plate
1989-91 240SX (A/T)	A/T slips, won't move in Reverse or makes noise	**91 74;** replace rear carrier assembly

NISSAN (cont'd)

Year and Model	Problem	TSB Number and Repair
1989-92 Maxima; 1990-92 Stanza (M/T)	Vibration or pulsation in pedal when releasing clutch	93-13; replace clutch release lever
1990 300ZX (turbocharged engine and M/T)	Clutch slips or won't engage	90-108; replace clutch master cylinder
1990 Axxess (A/T)	Buzz from A/T when accelerating cold engine	89-171; replace torque converter
1990 Axxess (A/T)	A/T won't upshift after a stop or no kickdown gear	89-117; reroute throttle wire
1990-91 300ZX (M/T)	Grind when shifting from fourth to fifth gear	91-86; replace Reverse gear
1990-91 Sentra and NX (M/T)	Difficulty shifting into Reverse	93-3; replace reverse idler gear
1990-91 300ZX (turbocharged engine and M/T)	Clutch slips	92-47; replace clutch master cylinder and return spring
1990-91 Pathfinder and light trucks (4-wheel drive)	Popping sound from below when accelerating from a stop	92-75; replace transfer case mainshaft
1990-92 Stanza (M/T)	Clutch noise when engaging first or Reverse gear	92-57; replace clutch disc
1990-92 300ZX (M/T)	Ringing sound in fifth gear only	92-82; replace Reverse gear
1990-92 300ZX (M/T)	Popping sound when activating clutch	92-18; overhaul clutch master cylinder
1990-91 light trucks (A/T)	Harsh 1-2 upshifts	91-62; remove orifice check valve and spring

NISSAN *(cont'd)*

Year and Model	Problem	TSB Number and Repair
1990-91 D21 light trucks (M/T)	Difficulty in shifting	**92-10;** analyze and repair according to service advisory
1991 300ZX, 240SX, Pathfinder, and light trucks (A/T)	A/T shifts erratically	**92-11;** analyze and repair according to service advisory
1991-92 240SX (M/T)	Vibration in fifth gear at 45–65 mph	**92-37;** replace overdrive gear
1991-92 240SX, 300ZX, light trucks (A/T)	A/T shifts harshly	**93-38;** replace shift solenoid and sensor
1991-92 Pathfinder and light trucks	Whine from rear at 25–45 mph	**92-67;** replace final drive
1992 240SX, 300ZX, Pathfinder	Differential fluid leak	**92-89;** replace drive pinion seal
1992 D21 light trucks (4-wheel drive)	Rattle from below	**92-119;** overhaul transfer case
1992 Sentra (A/T)	No upshifting from first gear	**92-26;** replace governor
1993 Quest XE and GXE (A/T)	Harsh, abrupt upshifts	**93-111;** replace control valve
1993 Quest (A/T)	Vibration or shudder during 1-2 upshifts	**93-39;** replace control valve

STEERING PROBLEMS

1988-93 240SX	Steering wheel vibration at 50–65 mph	**93-66;** analyze and repair according to service advisory
1989-91 Maxima	Car pulls to the side on a straight, flat road	**92-79;** analyze and repair according to service advisory
1989-91 Maxima; 1990-91 Stanza	Knock from steering column when wheel is turned	**93-101;** replace steering shaft

NISSAN (cont'd)

Year and Model	Problem	TSB Number and Repair
1990 300ZX	Car drifts to the side	**92-122;** replace front tires
1990-91 Stanza	Car pulls to the side	**92-80;** analyze and repair according to service advisory
1991-92 240SX	Car pulls to the side	**93-16;** analyze and repair according to service advisory

OLDSMOBILE

Year and Model	Problem	TSB Number and Repair

ENGINE PROBLEMS

Year and Model	Problem	TSB Number and Repair
1988-91 Cutlass Calais; 1990-91 Cutlass Supreme (2.3 engine)	Loss of coolant and white exhaust smoke	**91-T-244A;** replace cylinder head gasket
1988-92 Cutlass Calais, Achieva, Cutlass Ciera, Cutlass Supreme, Eighty Eight, Ninety Eight, Toronado, Bravada, Silhouette	Engine stalls, hesitates on acceleration, or loses power the first five minutes after a cold start	**92-T-117;** analyze and repair according to service advisory
1988-92 Eighty Eight and Ninety Eight	Loss of power or hesitation when making right-hand turns	**92-T-114;** replace fuel pump strainer
1988-92 models with V6 engine	Oil leak	**92-T-79;** replace rear main bearing seal
1988-93 Eighty Eight, Ninety Eight, Toronado; 1989-93 Cutlass Ciera, Cutlass	Hard starting or stalling on deceleration	**93-T-4;** replace idle air control

OLDSMOBILE *(cont'd)*

Year and Model	Problem	TSB Number and Repair
Cruiser, Cutlass Calais, Achieva; 1991-93 Silhouette (3.8 or 3800 engine)		
1990 Silhouette (3.1 engine)	Cold engine knock	**90-T-211;** replace engine or pistons
1989-90 Ninety Eight, Toronado, Trofeo; 1989-91 Eighty Eight (3.8 or 3800 engine)	Cold engine stalls when started or shudders at 35–45 mph	**91-T-185A;** replace memory and calibration (MEMCAL) unit
1989-90 Cutlass Supreme; 1990 Silhouette (3.1 engine)	Cold engine knocks in cold weather	**90-T-208;** replace engine block
1990 Cutlass Supreme (2.3 engine)	SERVICE ENGINE SOON light glows	**90-T-209;** replace spark knock sensor connector terminal
1990-91 Cutlass Supreme (3.1 engine)	Oil leak	**91-T-117;** seal intake manifold
1990-91 Cutlass Calais (2.5 engine and A/T)	Engine pings	**91-T-192A;** replace programmable read-only memory (PROM)
1990-92 Toronado and Trofeo	Engine occasionally won't start	**92-T-15;** replace starter interrupt relay
1990-92 Cutlass Supreme (3.1 or 3.4 engine)	Engine stalls when cold	**92-T-138;** replace memory and calibration (MEMCAL) unit
1991 Cutlass Calais and Cutlass Supreme (A/T)	Engine surges when decelerating or when on cruise control	**91-T-111;** replace A/T governor
1991 Custom Cruiser, Bravada, Silhouette	SERVICE ENGINE SOON light glows and engine may idle roughly	**91-T-171;** replace throttle position sensor

OLDSMOBILE *(cont'd)*

Year and Model	Problem	TSB Number and Repair
1991 Custom Cruiser (5.0 engine)	Engine performs poorly at low speed, may be hard to start, pings, backfires, or hesitates	91-T-129; replace programmable read-only memory (PROM)
1991 Silhouette	Lack of power	91-T-95; replace electronic spark control module
1991 Bravada	SERVICE ENGINE SOON light glows for no apparent reason	91-T-44; analyze and repair according to service advisory
1991 Custom Cruiser, Bravada, Silhouette, Cutlass Supreme (3.1 engine)	Engine is hard starting and may make a grinding or clashing sound	91-T-76; replace starter motor drive
1991 Custom Cruiser	Blue exhaust smoke	91-T-224; replace valve stem seals
1991 Ninety Eight and Toronado	Oil leaks after changing oil	91-T-144; install oil drip pan
1991 Cutlass Calais (3.3 engine)	Engine idles roughly or shudders on acceleration from a stop	91-T-94; replace engine mount
1991 Bravada (4.3 engine)	Engine shakes at low speed or while idling	91-T-218; realign engine
1991-93 Cutlass Supreme (3.1 or 3.4 engine)	Starter motor clicks, but occasionally engine won't crank	93-T-85; rewire theft alarm
1991 Cutlass Calais; 1992-93 Achieva (3.3 or 3300 engine)	Engine stalls on cold start	93-T-36; replace programmable read-only memory (PROM)
1991-92 Custom Cruiser (5.0 or 5.7 engine)	Engine pings or lacks power at low speed	92-T-68A; replace programmable read-only memory (PROM)

OLDSMOBILE *(cont'd)*

Year and Model	Problem	TSB Number and Repair
1991-92 Ninety Eight; 1992 Eighty Eight	Engine occasionally won't start	**92-T-99;** analyze and repair according to service advisory
1991-92 Ninety Eight, Toronado, Trofeo; 1992 Eighty Eight (3.8 or 3800 engine)	Engine stalls on cold start	**92-T-43;** replace memory and calibration (MEMCAL) unit
1992 Achieva (3.3 or 3300 engine)	Engine knocks	**92-T-171;** replace engine splash shield
1992 Achieva (3.3 or 3300 engine)	Engine stalls on cold start	**92-T-39;** replace memory and calibration (MEMCAL) unit
1992 Cutlass Ciera	Engine overheats	**92-T-4;** clean cooling system
1992 Custom Cruiser (5.7 engine and A/T)	Cold engine knocks	**92-T-173;** replace engine
1992 Achieva (2.3 engine)	Warm engine knocks	**92-T-81;** replace intake camshaft housing
1992 Custom Cruiser (5.0 or 5.7 engine)	Oil leak	**92-T-143;** replace camshaft plug
1992 Achieva	Warm engine stalls on deceleration	**92-T-106;** repair wire to idle air control
1992 Bravada (4.3 engine)	Engine tick or rattle when idling, or pings when accelerating	**92-T-111;** analyze and repair according to service advisory
1992 Achieva	Loss of power or hesitation on acceleration	**92-T-84;** replace fuel pump
1992 Custom Cruiser (5.0 or 5.7 engine); 1992 Achieva (2.3, 3.3, or 3300 engine)	Engine runs rough, misses, pings, hesitates, surges, stalls, or is hard to start	**92-T-127;** replace wire terminal connectors
1992-93 Achieva	Engine is hard to start or runs rough	**93-T-79;** reposition engine control module wire harness

OLDSMOBILE *(cont'd)*

Year and Model	Problem	TSB Number and Repair
1992-93 Ninety Eight Touring Sedan (3.8 supercharged engine)	Engine stalls on cold start	**93-T-32;** replace programmable read-only memory (PROM)
1992-93 Eighty Eight and Ninety Eight (3.8 or 3800 engine)	Engine misfires	**93-T-68;** replace spark plugs and spark plug cables
1992-93 Cutlass Ciera, Cutlass Cruiser, Eighty Eight, Ninety Eight Touring Sedan, Toronado, Achieva, Silhouette (3.3, 3.8, 3800, or 3.8 supercharged engine)	Engine knocks	**93-T-59;** replace main bearings
1993 Bravada (4.3 engine)	Engine knocks	**93-T-73;** replace engine

BRAKING PROBLEMS

Year and Model	Problem	TSB Number and Repair
1988-90 Eighty Eight, Ninety Eight, Toronado	ABS pump fails	**90-T-212;** replace ABS pump relay
1988-93 Cutlass Supreme	Brakes are noisy or pads wear out prematurely	**93-T-52;** install improved pads
1990-91 Cutlass Calais; 1990-92 Eighty Eight and Ninety Eight; 1992 Achieva	Poor braking or noise when applying brake pedal	**92-T-18;** replace caliper parts
1991 Eighty Eight and Ninety Eight	Rear brake shoes freeze to drums in cold weather	**91-T-146;** replace shoes
1991-92 Eighty Eight and Ninety Eight (ABS)	Pedal pulsates when braking	**92-T-121;** replace wheel speed sensor

OLDSMOBILE *(cont'd)*

Year and Model	Problem	TSB Number and Repair
1991-93 Ninety Eight; 1992-93 Eighty Eight (ABS)	ABS warning light glows	93-T-71; analyze and repair according to service advisory
1992 Eighty Eight and Ninety Eight	Noise from rear when braking, one rear wheel slides, or excessive brake pedal travel	92-T-147; replace parking brake adjuster spring
1992-93 Silhouette	ABS warning light glows and rear wheel won't turn in cold weather when starting from a parked position	93-T-14; replace rear brake linings
1992-93 Achieva	Noise when braking to a stop	93-T-29; replace rear brake linings
1993 Cutlass Ciera and Cutlass Cruiser	Brakes drag, causing loss of power or inability to engage cruise control	93-T-25; overhaul brake booster

TRANSMISSION AND DIFFERENTIAL PROBLEMS

1988-90 Ninety Eight Touring Sedan	Difficulty shifting into Park or removing ignition key from lock with shift lever in Park	90-T-198; analyze and repair according to service advisory
1988-91 models with 4L60 A/T	No third or fourth gear	91-T-196; analyze and repair according to service advisory
1988-92 models with 4T60 A/T	Harsh 3-2 downshifts	92-T-69; analyze and repair according to service advisory
1989-91 Cutlass Ciera and Cutlass Supreme (2.8 or 3.1 engine and A/T)	A/T slips or bumps on 3-2 downshifts	91-T-66; analyze and repair according to service advisory
1990-91 Cutlass Supreme (3.1 engine and A/T)	Delayed upshifts	91-T-63; adjust throttle valve cable

OLDSMOBILE *(cont'd)*

Year and Model	Problem	TSB Number and Repair
1991 Cutlass Ciera, Cutlass Supreme, Eighty Eight (A/T)	Transmission fluid leak	**91-T-225;** replace transmission case
1991 Cutlass Supreme (3.4 engine and M/T)	Bump sensation when decelerating	**91-T-230;** install clutch anticipate kit
1991 Bravada and Custom Cruiser (A/T)	A/T sticks in Reverse	**91-T-115;** repair control valve
1991 Bravada and Custom Cruiser (A/T)	No or delayed Reverse in cold weather	**91-T-238A;** replace reverse input clutch piston seal
1991 Bravada and Custom Cruiser (A/T)	A/T gets stuck in first gear and won't upshift	**91-T-170;** overhaul transmission
1991 Bravada	Constant velocity joint boot failure	**91-T-161;** install improved boots
1991 Eighty Eight and Ninety Eight (A/T)	Transmission fluid leak	**91-T-221;** replace transmission cooler hoses and install new clamp
1991-92 models with 4T60 and 4T60E A/T	Transmission fluid leak	**92-T-51A;** replace side cover pan
1991-92 Bravada (4.3 engine and A/T)	Transmission downshifts sluggishly or not at all	**92-T-37;** replace accelerator cable
1991-93 Bravada	Differential grease leak	**93-T-69;** replace front axle driveshaft
1991-93 models with 4T60E A/T	Transmission fluid leak	**93-T-21A;** replace helix converter seal
1992 Bravada and Custom Cruiser (A/T)	Harsh 1-2 upshifts	**92-T-137;** replace accumulator valve and sleeve

OLDSMOBILE *(cont'd)*

Year and Model	Problem	TSB Number and Repair
1992 Eighty Eight and Ninety Eight (A/T)	Harsh 1-2 upshifts or 2-1 downshifts, or lack of Drive or Reverse	**92-T-83;** repair transmission control valve
1992-93 models with 3T40 A/T	No Reverse or A/T slips in Reverse	**93-T-9;** replace Reverse clutch return spring

STEERING PROBLEMS

Year and Model	Problem	TSB Number and Repair
1988-91 Cutlass Calais; 1992 Achieva	Car pulls to side and abnormal tire wear	**92-T-20;** analyze and repair according to service advisory
1988-91 all models	Loss of power steering in cold weather	**91-T-79;** install low temperature power steering fluid
1990-92 Toronado and Trofeo	Car pulls to left at highway speed	**92-T-101;** reinforce transaxle mount
1992 Achieva	Car pulls to side after straightening out from a turn	**92-T-100;** replace upper strut bearing
1991-92 Ninety Eight; 1992 Eighty Eight	Car pulls to side on acceleration	**92-T-5;** install torque strut
1992-93 Achieva	Car pulls to side on smooth, flat road	**93-T-60;** replace strut mounts

PONTIAC

Year and Model	Problem	TSB Number and Repair

ENGINE PROBLEMS

Year and Model	Problem	TSB Number and Repair
1988-91 Grand Am and Grand Prix (Quad 4 engine)	White exhaust smoke or loss of coolant	**91-6-54;** replace cylinder head gasket
1988-01 Firebird and Grand Prix (5.0 or 5.7 engine)	Blue exhaust smoke when starting	**91-6-55;** replace valve stem seals

PONTIAC (cont'd)

Year and Model	Problem	TSB Number and Repair
1988-92 Bonneville	Loss of power or hesitation when making right turns	92-6-55; replace fuel pump strainer
1988-93 Bonneville (3800 engine); 1992-93 Grand Am (3300 engine); 1992-93 Trans Sport (3800 engine)	Engine stalls on deceleration or is hard to start	93-6-5; replace idle air control motor
1989-90 Bonneville (3800 engine)	Engine is hard to start	90-6-14; replace memory and calibration (MEMCAL) unit
1989-90 Bonneville (3800 engine)	Oil leak	90-6-44A; replace oil pan
1989-90 Bonneville	Engine misses at high speed	90-6-41; replace camshaft
1989-90 Grand Am or Grand Prix (2.3 engine)	Engine misses or loses power	90-6-30; replace fuel injector
1989-91 Bonneville (3800 engine)	Cold engine stalls when started	91-6-49; replace memory and calibration (MEMCAL) unit
1989-91 Sunbird (2.0 engine and A/T)	Cold engine stalls or hesitates	91-6-61A; replace intake manifold and programmable read-only memory (PROM)
1990 Grand Am (2.3 engine)	Engine won't start or stalls	90-6-26; repair wires
1990 Trans Sport	Poor fuel economy	90-6-42; replace fuel tank and fuel tank sender
1990 Trans Sport (3.1 engine)	Engine knocks when cold	90-6-52B; replace engine block
1990 Firebird (3.1 engine and A/T)	Cold engine stalls	90-6-31; replace memory and calibration (MEMCAL) unit

PONTIAC *(cont'd)*

Year and Model	Problem	TSB Number and Repair
1990-91 LeMans (1.6 engine)	Poor performance	**91-6-39;** replace memory and calibration (MEMCAL) unit
1990-91 Grand Am (2.5 engine and A/T)	Engine pings	**91-6-59;** replace programmable read-only memory (PROM)
1990-91 Grand Am (2.5 engine)	Loss of coolant	**91-6-44;** replace lower radiator hose
1990-91 6000, Sunbird, Grand Prix (3.1 engine)	Oil leak	**91-6-38;** reseal intake manifold, cylinder head, and cylinder block
1990-91 Firebird (5.0 engine)	Engine idles rough or stalls when coming to a stop	**91-6-2A;** replace memory and calibration (MEMCAL) unit and install knock sensor
1990-91 Firebird (5.0 or 5.7 engine)	Rough idle, hesitation, missing, surging, or blown fuses	**91-8-4;** repair wires
1990-92 LeMans (1.6 engine)	Engine won't start because battery keeps running down	**92-6-42;** replace alternator bracket fasteners
1990-92 Bonneville	Engine occasionally fails to crank	**92-8-21;** replace starter enable relay
1990-92 Sunbird and Grand Prix (3.1 or 3.4 engine)	Stalling	**92-6-60A;** replace memory and calibration (MEMCAL) unit
1990-92 Firebird (3.1 engine)	Cold engine stalls, hesitates, or idles rough	**92-6-44;** replace high-energy ignition module
1991 Sunbird, Grand Am, Grand Prix (A/T)	Engine surges on deceleration or with cruise control on	**91-7-29;** replace A/T governor
1991 Sunbird, Grand Prix, Firebird (3.1 or 5.0 engine)	Engine is hard to start or makes grinding noise during attempted starts	**91-6-22;** replace starter motor drive

PONTIAC *(cont'd)*

Year and Model	Problem	TSB Number and Repair
1991 Firebird (5.0 engine)	Engine hesitates at slow speed, surges when idling, or idles rough	**91-6-4;** replace throttle position sensor
1991-92 6000, Sunbird, Grand Am, Grand Prix, Sunbird, Bonneville, Firebird; 1992 Trans Sport	Cold engine stalls, hesitates, or loses power	**92-6-49;** analyze and repair according to service advisory
1991-92 Firebird (5.0 engine)	Hesitates or stalls when stopping; results in hard restarting in hot weather	**92-6-67;** replace fuel pump and sender
1991-92 Firebird	Engine idles poorly	**92-6-2B;** replace throttle position sensor
1991-92 Firebird	Engine loses coolant without showing visible signs of a leak	**92-6-16;** replace cylinder heads
1991-93 Grand Prix (3.1 or 3.4 engine)	Starter clicks; on occasion, engine won't crank	**93-8-23;** rewire theft alarm
1992 Sunbird (2.0 engine)	Engine consumes too much oil	**92-6-29;** replace PCV hose
1992 Sunbird and Grand Am	Engine performs sluggishly, hesitates, or loses power	**92-6-39;** replace fuel pump
1992 Grand Am (2.3 engine and A/T)	Warm engine knocks when idling	**92-6-41;** replace camshaft housing
1992 Grand Am	Engine rocks back and forth, leaks coolant, or makes noise	**92-6-48A;** replace engine mount lower strut
1992 Grand Am (2.3 or 3300 engine)	Reduced fuel economy, rough running, or missing	**92-6-58;** repair electronic control module terminals

PONTIAC *(cont'd)*

Year and Model	Problem	TSB Number and Repair
1992 Grand Am (2.3 engine)	Warm engine stalls on deceleration	**92-6-52;** repair idle air control wires
1991 Bonneville (column shift lever)	Engine won't start because battery runs down on occasion	**92-8-28;** replace brake transmission shift interlock solenoid
1992 Bonneville (3800 engine)	Cold engine stalls	**92-6-22;** replace memory and calibration (MEMCAL) unit
1992 Firebird (5.0 or 5.7 engine)	Oil leak	**92-6-64;** reseal camshaft plug
1992-93 Sunbird (2.0 engine)	Loss of coolant	**93-6-27;** replace coolant pump
1992-93 Grand Am (3300 engine)	Cold engine stalls when started	**93-6-19;** replace memory and calibration (MEMCAL) unit
1992-93 Grand Am	Engine is hard to start or runs rough	**93-8-20;** reposition engine wire harness
1992-93 Bonneville (3800 engine and supercharger)	Engine misfires	**93-6-38;** replace spark plugs and spark plug cables
1992-93 Bonneville, Grand Am, Grand Prix, Trans Sport (3300, 3800, or 3800 supercharged engine)	Engine knocks	**93-6-34;** replace main bearings
1992-93 Bonneville (3800 engine and supercharger)	Cold engine stalls	**93-6-23;** replace programmable read-only memory (PROM)

BRAKING PROBLEMS

1988-92 Grand Prix; 1990-91 Trans Sport	Rattle or buzz when applying or releasing brake pedal	**92-5-12;** replace brake booster check valve

PONTIAC (cont'd)

Year and Model	Problem	TSB Number and Repair
1988-93 Grand Prix	Squeal when applying brakes, reduced brake pad life, or brake pedal is too firm	93-5-9A; replace pads
1990-92 Firebird	Parking brake lever slips when applied	92-5-13; replace parking brake hand lever assembly
1991-92 Grand Am; 1992 Sunbird	ABS warning light glows for no apparent reason	92-5-21; replace brake electronic control module
1991-92 Bonneville	Rear brake linings freeze to drums temporarily in cold weather	92-5-10; replace rear brake shoes
1991-92 Bonneville	Brake pedal vibrates and falls away when pressed	92-5-19; replace rear wheel speed sensors
1991-93 Bonneville	ABS warning light glows	93-5-14; replace pressure modulator valve
1992 Bonneville	Buzz when brakes are applied	92-5-9; replace ABS pressure modulator valve bracket
1992 Bonneville and Trans Sport	Noise from rear, or rear wheel slides when brakes are applied, or excessive brake pedal travel	92-5-22A; replace rear parking brake adjuster spring
1992-93 Sunbird and Grand Am	Squawk or ABS cycles when brakes are applied	93-5-5; replace rear brake linings and service drums
1992-93 Trans Sport	ABS warning light glows and rear brake shoes freeze to drums temporarily in cold weather	93-5-3; replace rear brake shoes
1993 Firebird	Moan when applying brakes	93-5-8; replace caliper dampers

PONTIAC *(cont'd)*

Year and Model	Problem	TSB Number and Repair
TRANSMISSION AND DIFFERENTIAL PROBLEMS		
1991 Sunbird, Grand Am, Grand Prix (A/T)	A/T doesn't upshift	**91-7-29;** replace governor
1991 Bonneville, Grand Prix, 6000 (A/T)	A/T fluid leak	**91-7-41;** replace A/T case
1991 Bonneville (A/T)	Difficulty shifting out of Park	**91-7-22;** adjust brake trans-axle shift interlock
1991 Bonneville	A/T fluid leak	**91-7-40;** reinforce A/T cooler lines
1991 Grand Prix (A/T)	Erratic A/T perfor-mance and lack of speedometer reading	**91-7-16;** replace speed sen-sor
1991-92 Bonneville, Grand Prix, Trans Sport (A/T)	Delayed engagement into Drive or Reverse	**92-7-4;** replace input clutch outer seal
1991-92 Bonneville, Grand Prix, Trans Sport (A/T)	A/T fluid leak	**92-7-10;** replace side cover pan
1991-93 Bonneville, Grand Prix, Trans Sport (A/T)	A/T fluid leak	**93-7-8A;** replace A/T
1991-93 Bonneville, 6000, Grand Prix, Trans Sport (A/T)	Whine from transmis-sion in first, second, and third gear	**93-7-25;** replace bearing as-sembly in A/T
1992 Bonneville, Grand Prix, Trans Sport (A/T)	A/T shifts erratically	**92-7-11;** replace solenoid
1992 Bonneville, Grand Prix, Trans Sport (A/T)	A/T shifts erratically or engine can be started in second or third gear	**92-7-17;** analyze and repair according to service advisory

PONTIAC *(cont'd)*

Year and Model	Problem	TSB Number and Repair
1992 Grand Am (2.3 engine and 5-speed M/T)	Fluid level indicator shows extreme overfill or underfill condition	**92-7-19;** replace fluid level indicator
1992 Firebird (A/T)	Harsh 1-2 upshifts	**92-7-20;** replace 1-2 accumulator sleeve
1992 Firebird (5.0 engine and 5-speed M/T)	Premature clutch failure	**92-7-24;** replace clutch driven disc and clutch cover
1992-93 Sunbird, Grand Am, Grand Prix, Trans Sport (A/T)	A/T slips in Reverse or lacks Reverse	**93-7-3;** replace low and Reverse clutch return spring
1993 Grand Am (2.3 engine and A/T)	Torque converter clutch is slow to apply or doesn't apply	**93-7-6;** replace auxiliary valve body gasket
1993 Bonneville and Trans Sport (A/T)	Torque converter clutch is slow to apply or doesn't apply	**93-7-17;** replace pulse width modulator solenoid
1993 Firebird (5.7 engine and A/T)	Clunk when coasting from 3-2 downshifts	**93-7-21A;** replace valve body spacer plate

STEERING PROBLEMS

1990-91 6000	Steering vibration or moan with car at standstill or moving at slow speed	**91-3-25;** replace power steering hose and pipe assembly
1990-91 Trans Sport	Steering wheel oscillates	**91-3-17;** replace steering gear adjuster spring
1990-92 Trans Sport (3.1 engine)	Steering vibration or moan with car at standstill or moving at slow speed	**92-3-14;** replace power steering hose and pipe assembly
1991-92 Bonneville	Car wheel pulls to side	**92-6-12;** replace rear torque strut

PONTIAC *(cont'd)*

Year and Model	Problem	TSB Number and Repair
1992-93 Grand Am	Car wheel pulls to side	93-3-10; replace upper strut mounts

TOYOTA

Year and Model	Problem	TSB Number and Repair

ENGINE PROBLEMS

1988-90 Camry and Celica (3S-FE engine)	Cold engine knocks	Vol. 10, No. 28, Engine; replace pistons
1988-91 Camry	Poor driveability as engine is warming up	EN91-004; replace engine control module
1988-91 Tercel (3E engine)	Excessive oil consumption	EN91-003; replace valve stem seals
1990-91 Tercel	CHECK ENGINE light glows for no apparent reason	EN91-010; replace engine control module
1990-93 Camry, Celica, MR2 (5S-FE engine and A/T)	Engine hesitates on acceleration from 45 to 60 mph	EG93-001; replace EGR vacuum modulator
1991-92 Camry	Thump from engine at 5 mph or less	EN91-13; replace main journal bearing
1991-93 4Runner and light trucks (M/T)	Engine hesitates or misses on downhill grades	EG93-2; replace engine control module
1993 Camry (3VZ-FE engine)	Warm engine is hard to start or misses on downhill grades	EG92-4; replace engine control module

BRAKING PROBLEMS

1989-91 4Runner and 4×4 light trucks	Vibration when applying brakes	Vol. 10, No. 12, Brakes; replace drums

TOYOTA *(cont'd)*

Year and Model	Problem	TSB Number and Repair
1990-91 4Runner and light trucks (ABS)	ABS warning light glows for no apparent reason	**BK91-2;** replace ABS electronic control unit
1990-91 Camry (ABS)	Squeak from front when applying brakes	**BK91-4;** replace front rotors
1991 MR2	Squeak from front when applying brakes	**Vol. 10, No. 9, Brakes;** replace front springs
1992 Camry (ABS)	Squeak from rear when applying brakes	**BR92-2;** replace rear pads

TRANSMISSION AND DIFFERENTIAL PROBLEMS

Year and Model	Problem	TSB Number and Repair
1990-91 Camry, Celica, Cressida, Tercel, MR2 (A/T)	Harsh disengagement shifting from Drive to Neutral	**TM91-6;** replace forward clutch return spring assembly
1990-92 MR2 (M/T)	Difficulty shifting from second to third gear	**TC92-3;** overhaul M/T
1990-93 Camry (A/T)	Delay in shifts with cold engine	**TC93-4;** repair valve body
1991-92 Previa (A/T)	Harsh 1-2 upshifts	**TM91-21;** replace valve body

PART II

Government-Mandated Free Car Repairs:

SAFETY RECALLS

THE NATIONAL TRAFFIC AND MOTOR VEHICLE SAFETY Act, which was passed by Congress and signed into law by President Lyndon B. Johnson in 1966, established the safety recall program. Since then, auto manufacturers have recalled approximately 150 million motor vehicles to repair safety-related manufacturing defects and design flaws. With recalls, repairs are done at no cost to vehicle owners.

According to the National Highway Traffic Safety Administration (NHTSA), which oversees the recall program, approximately 35 percent of the vehicle owners who receive or should receive notices calling for free repairs do not have them made. Therefore, there are millions of vehicles presently on the road that have defects—each defect could cost an owner hundreds or thousands of dollars to fix—that could conceivably be repaired for free under the safety recall program of the federal government.

Unfortunately, some problems are not perceived by car owners as safety hazards. For example, an engine that consumes oil, a transmission that makes a whining sound, and a body panel that is rusting are not considered safety-related problems by most car owners. Usually, only when a problem becomes serious enough do car owners bring their vehicles to mechanics and pay to have repairs made, when, in fact, repairs could have been made earlier by vehicle manufacturers at no cost to car owners.

DEFICIENCIES IN NOTIFICATION SYSTEM

The law requires that manufacturers send notices of safety recalls to registered owners of affected cars by first-class mail. Most of the people who unwittingly pay for repairs that could have been made for free are owners of used cars whose previous owners may have received notices but did not follow through on the repairs. There are also those people who buy new cars and don't receive notification of recalls—the notification system is not foolproof. In both situations, owners end up paying for repairs that should have been made free of charge.

For example, in 1989 the Ford Motor Company issued a recall on 481,000 1984 and 1985 Ford Escort and Mercury Lynx models because the cylinder head had the potential for cracking and allowing oil to leak from the engine to a hot exhaust manifold, where it might start a fire. Under the terms of the recall, Ford will install a new cylinder head at no cost to the owner.

Suppose you buy one of these cars from a used car dealer, and the previous owner didn't bother to have the repair made. Or say you bought the car new but the recall notice you should have received never arrived. Maybe it was lost in the mail, or maybe you moved and didn't leave a forwarding address. In any case, low oil dipstick readings indicate that the engine is consuming or losing oil. This is not a situation that would cause most of us to think that a safety-related defect exists.

Carrying the scenario one step further, let's say you bring the car to a mechanic who tells you that the reason for the loss of oil is a cracked cylinder head. As a result, you could end up paying $400 to have a new cylinder head installed, never realizing that Ford Motor Company would have installed the part for you for nothing because of the recall.

Another example of a problem that could needlessly cost owners money involves 1985 to 1991 Audis. In 1993, recall notices were mailed to 152,000 owners of these cars because the oil (installed at the factory) to lubricate the differential had a lower-than-normal tolerance to heat and was evaporating. (The differential is the assembly that transmits power from the engine and transmission to the drive wheels.) If forced to operate on a reduced supply of oil, the bearings and gears inside the differential could eventually fail, causing the drive wheels to lock and toss a moving car into a spin. Audi and NHTSA auto engineers considered this a safety-related condition that required a recall.

The solution to the problem provided by the recall is to drain the old oil from the differential and install a superior grade of lubricant. Since it comes under the provisions of the government-mandated safety recall program, the service is to be done at Audi dealerships and paid for by Volkswagen of America, which manufactures the Audi.

According to NHTSA's 35 percent noncompliance estimate, there are approximately 53,000 Audis that have not had this service performed and are candidates for a differential breakdown. Suppose you buy one of these cars. Would it ever occur to you to check on the possibility that a safety recall exists covering the oil in the differential?

Suppose you don't check. Then a few months after purchasing the car, you begin hearing a loud whirring noise. A trip to the service department of an Audi dealership reveals that the differential gears and bearings are shot and an overhaul is needed. By then it's too late for you to do anything about it, even if you are told that a safety-related recall is in effect. The recall covers the cost of replacing the oil that could have prevented the failure. It doesn't cover the cost of rebuilding the differential, which is approximately $800.

USING THE ACT

Two points to keep in mind about government-mandated safety recalls and free repairs are these:

1. If you buy a used car, check to see if a safety recall is in effect. If one is, get the repair done by the service department of a new car dealer that sells the particular make of vehicle.
2. If you buy a new car and a problem develops after the warranty expires, find out whether a safety recall has been announced, even if the problem you're having doesn't seem to have any relation to safety. Don't take it for granted that you would have gotten a notice from the manufacturer. It could have gone astray.

Whether your car is new or used, it is wise to check periodically—at least once a year—to find out if a safety recall has been announced for your car. Don't rely on the notification system. And don't rely on the media. Most recalls involve a few thousand cars; only the recalls that involve hundreds of thousands or millions of cars usually make news.

FINDING A RECALL

To find out if you've missed a safety recall that applies to your car, have the dealership check its computer records or call NHTSA's toll-free hotline number, which is 800-424-9393 (or 366-0123 if you reside in the District of Columbia). Car recalls are also published in *Consumer Reports* magazine.

If there's been a recall for your car's make and model, NHTSA will send you a request-for-information card, preaddressed with the name and address of the vehicle manufacturer. When it arrives, fill in the data. You'll need the vehicle identification number (VIN), which you can get from the car registration, insurance identification card, or from the plate mounted to the forward part of the dashboard where it meets the windshield on the driver's side. The manufacturer will let you know if the recall applies to your particular vehicle, and, if so, whether the repair has been made to your car already (if you bought the car used).

STATUTE OF LIMITATIONS

The offer of a free repair for a recalled vehicle extends eight years from the date the recall is announced. If you find out that your car has been recalled but the time allowed by law to have the free repair made has elapsed, don't give up. Car manufacturers have goodwill policy programs. Repairs called for by expired recalls may still be paid for, at least in part, by the manufacturer. Therefore, contact a dealer to get in touch with the manufacturer. Don't accept the dealer's word if you are told there is no goodwill policy. Demand to speak with a field representative or with someone in authority working in the manufacturer's customer service department. If the dealer won't follow through on your request, go to another dealer. If no one is responsive, contact the customer service department yourself. Addresses and telephone numbers of manufacturers are listed in Appendix I.

PART III

Government-Mandated Free Car Repairs:

EMISSIONS RECALLS

IN ADDITION TO SAFETY RECALLS, THERE IS ANOTHER recall program that has been mandated by Congress that you can use to get your vehicle fixed free. Established by the National Clean Air Act, this program's purpose is to correct defects that cause engines to expel excessive amounts of carbon monoxide, hydrocarbons, and oxides of nitrogen into the atmosphere. The free repairs made by a manufacturer to prevent air pollution will usually correct a performance problem—hard starting, hesitation, misfiring, surging, rough idling, lack of power, pinging, backfire, and abnormal fuel consumption—that a customer may be having with a car's engine.

PERFORMANCE PROBLEMS DEFINED

Hard starting occurs when the engine cranks normally but doesn't start promptly. Or the engine may start promptly but stalls almost as soon as it gets going or when you shift the transmission into gear.

Hesitation, which is also called *sag* or *stumble,* describes a lack of response from the engine as you press the accelerator pedal to get going from a standstill or to increase driving speed—for example, to pass another car. There is a momentary flat spot.

Misfiring is a pulsation that's felt when the engine is running at a slow rate of speed. Usually, the pulsation is not felt when driving above 30 miles per hour.

Surging refers to a variation in engine speed that occurs despite a steady foot on the accelerator pedal. Although you don't vary the pressure on the pedal, the engine alternately speeds up and slows down as if it can't make up its mind.

Rough idling occurs when the engine fails to run at a consistent speed, causing the car to shake while it's standing still. If the condition is severe enough, the engine will stall.

Lack of power occurs when you don't get the power you expect when accelerating. There is little or no increase in speed when you press down on the accelerator pedal.

Pinging, which is also called *spark knock, auto-ignition,* or *detonation,* is a metallic sound that comes from the engine. It usually gets worse as you accelerate but tapers off as you ease up on the accelerator pedal.

Backfire occurs when fuel ignites in the intake manifold or the exhaust system because of a leaking intake or exhaust valve. It is characterized by a loud popping noise.

Abnormal fuel consumption occurs when the engine uses more gasoline than it should. If there is one condition that characterizes high exhaust emissions, it is this one. When a vehicle is recalled to correct an engine that produces high levels of hydrocarbons and/or carbon monoxide, that engine is consuming too much gasoline and is probably also demonstrating one of the other performance problems.

THE UNNECESSARY COST OF POOR PERFORMANCE

The Environmental Protection Agency (EPA), which oversees the clean-air recall program, estimates that car owners unnecessarily pay millions of dollars for repairing poor performance problems because they don't heed exhaust emissions recall notices.

Either they disregard the notices, don't receive the notices because of a postal or administrative error, or don't relate the engine performance problem they're having to a recall for high emissions.

For example, General Motors recalled 377,000 1987 to 1990 models to correct a malfunction that causes the 2.3-liter Quad Four engines to emit excessive amounts of hydrocarbons and carbon monoxide. The defect also causes misfiring.

Misfiring occurs when gasoline in one of the cylinders doesn't ignite. The unburned gasoline is thrown out the tailpipe, resulting in high emissions and poor gas mileage. Usually, a car owner doesn't investigate an exhaust emissions recall when an engine begins to misfire. Instead, the car is brought to a mechanic for repair. In the case of the Quad Four engine, it would cost the owner about $125 to replace a cracked ignition coil. Under the terms of the recall, GM will install the new coil for free.

POINTS TO KEEP IN MIND

Unlike a safety recall, which has an eight-year statute of limitations, an exhaust emissions recall remains in effect for the life of the car. Therefore, this program has nothing to do with the five-year or 50,000-mile new car emissions control systems warranty described in part IV. If a problem develops after this warranty expires, there is no obligation on the part of the manufacturer to fix it for free. On the other hand, if your car is recalled for an emissions condition, accompanied by an engine performance problem, it will be fixed free regardless of time elapsed.

ERRONEOUS STATE INSPECTION TEST

There is another point to keep in mind about exhaust emissions that could save you money. If the state in which you reside is like most states, it requires an exhaust emissions inspection before vehicle registration is renewed. If your car fails an inspection, don't make any repairs without having the car reinspected.

Some exhaust emissions control systems are supposed to be inactive when the engine isn't fully warmed up or if it exceeds the temperature range that is considered normal. Excessive exhaust emissions may result if, for example, you have to wait too long on an inspection line with the engine running at idle speed. Consequently, the car may fail inspection although there's nothing wrong with it.

If you have to wait on line longer than 10 minutes, bring engine temperature down to a more normal level just before the inspection is done by shifting the transmission into Park or Neutral and depressing the accelerator pedal to bring the engine speed up to a level that is equal to a driving speed of 55 to 60 miles per hour. Run the engine at this speed for at least a minute before the inspection, keeping your other foot firmly on the brake pedal.

FINDING A RELEVANT RECALL

To find out if your vehicle is included in an exhaust emissions recall, ask a new car dealer who sells your make of car to enter the vehicle identification number (VIN) into the computer tied into the manufacturer's recall databank. The computer will reveal if an exhaust emissions recall has been announced for your vehicle.

You can also request this information from the customer service department of the manufacturer or by writing to the Manufacturing Operations Division, Environmental Protection Agency, 401 M Street, SW, Washington, DC 20460. The phone number is 202-260-2479. Be sure to provide the VIN. With information about an exhaust emissions recall in hand, take the vehicle to a new car dealer who sells your make of car and have the free repair done.

PART IV

Using Warranties to Get

FREE REPAIRS
YOU'RE ENTITLED TO RECEIVE

Nᴇᴡ Cᴀʀs Cᴏᴍᴇ Wɪᴛʜ As Mᴀɴʏ As Sᴇᴠᴇɴ warranties, usually referred to as basic, power-train, emissions control systems, rust-through, tire, battery, and supplemental inflatable restraint (air bag). In recent years, manufacturers have clumped together the basic and power-train warranties into a single package called "bumper-to-bumper."

Some warranties, specifically those required by federal law, are automatically transferred to people who buy cars in used condition. Others can be transferred to a buyer of a used car if the manufacturer permits, but a transfer fee may be charged.

Important: In recent years, some manufacturers have eased restrictions on warranties for second and subsequent parties. The complete warranty package will automatically be applied to a car at no charge. If you're buying a used vehicle, ask about this or contact the customer service department of the particular manufacturer (see Appendix I) to determine which warranties, if any, are applicable.

BASICS ABOUT "BASICS"

A basic warranty or the basic part of a bumper-to-bumper warranty normally runs for a vehicle's first 12 months or 12,000 miles, whichever occurs first. During that period, the repair of any flaw due to an error in manufacturing or a faulty part will be fully paid for by the manufacturer.

If the manufacturer of the car offers a power-train warranty, power-train coverage kicks in after the basic warranty period expires. The power-train warranty protects the car owner against engine, transmission, and differential failure as long as that failure is not caused by owner neglect or abuse of the vehicle, such as failing to follow manufacturer maintenance servicing requirements. Repairs are not normally free—you usually have to pay $50 or $100 for each.

The period of time that a power-train warranty remains in effect depends on the manufacturer. For less-expensive model cars, that period is generally 24 months or 24,000 miles, whichever occurs first, beyond the basic warranty period. The power-train warranties of some luxury model cars extend for 60 months or 88,000 miles, whichever occurs first, beyond the basic warranty period.

A bumper-to-bumper warranty covers the entire vehicle for an extended period. This includes a basic warranty period of 12 months or 12,000 miles, whichever occurs first, during which time the repair of every flaw and defect that is the fault of the manufacturer is paid for in full by the manufacturer. After that, repairs for anything resulting from a manufacturing deficiency or a defect in components—not only engine, transmission, and differential problems—are paid for on a shared basis. You usually have to pay $50 or $100 each time a repair is made, with the manufacturer paying the remainder.

Throughout the industry, the standard period of time bumper-to-bumper warranties are in effect (as of January 1994) was three years or 36,000 miles, whichever occurs first. The manufacturer of your car may be more generous. You can verify this by consulting the warranty booklet that comes with your car.

To summarize, the difference between a bumper-to-bumper warranty and a basic/power-train warranty package is that the former covers the entire car for an extended period. The latter covers the entire car for a short period and the engine, transmission, and differential for an extended period.

NOT 100 PERCENT FREE

On the surface, the extended period of a bumper-to-bumper warranty may look like a wonderful deal, but be careful. It may lull you into a sense of security that can end up needlessly costing you money if a dealer is dishonest.

Suppose the basic warranty on your car has expired when you spot a puddle of oil on the garage floor. You bring the car to a dealer service department and ask that it be repaired under the bumper-to-bumper warranty. The service manager may ask you to pay the $100 deductible, even when (unbeknownst to you) the repair involves simply tightening valve cover bolts. Some dealers will perform this five-minute repair for free; others will charge up to $25.

Or, the dealer may tell you that a valve cover gasket has to be replaced—a procedure that can cost as much as $200. The dealer may correct the problem by tightening the valve cover bolts and charging you the $100 "deductible." This, of course, is dishonest.

Most dealers don't engage in such practices. However, the best way to make sure you aren't blind-sided is to bring your car to the dealership where you bought it for all repairs that have to be made during the bumper-to-bumper warranty period. If this is not possible, find a dealer who sells your make of car and has been doing business in the community for a long time. You can check with the Better Business Bureau to determine whether any complaints have been lodged against a service department for this kind of double-dealing.

If you suspect that you've been conned by a service department, take the matter up with the owner of the dealership; then, if necessary, with the manufacturer.

MORE COVERAGE THAN YOU MIGHT THINK

If something goes wrong with a car during the time/mileage period that a basic/power-train or a bumper-to-bumper warranty is in effect, most owners know enough to return a car to the dealer they bought it from to get the car fixed free. Where many owners trip themselves up (and pay for needless repairs) is after the basic or bumper-to-bumper warranty expires. At this point, they believe they are responsible for paying to have any performance problem repaired. Performance problems, which usually affect driveability, include rough idling, engine misfire, loss of power, hard starting, hesitation, stalling, bucking, and a drastic drop in fuel economy.

When such a problem occurs, car owners should determine if the emissions systems warranties can be used to get the repair made for free. A performance problem and excessive emissions usually go hand-in-hand; thus, repairing the cause of the emissions problem will also correct the driveability problem. However, you must have proof that the emissions level exceeds federal or state standards before you can have the repair made at no cost.

HOW IT WORKS

Although referred to in the singular, technically there are two emissions systems warranties that come with every new vehicle. One is called "design and defect," the other "performance." Both are mandated by federal law and are intended to ensure that vehicles will not cause excessive air pollution. Their purpose is *not* to resolve a driveability problem for a car owner, but often these warranties have that result. Consider this scenario:

Suppose your car has been driven less than 50,000 miles and is less than five years old when it begins to buck severely as you attempt to accelerate. The condition is not just annoying—it is also dangerous (you may have to merge onto a busy interstate highway in the morning on your way to work). Therefore, you might take the car to a mechanic and pay to have the problem repaired.

Instead of scurrying to a repair shop, you take the car to a dealership that sells your make of vehicle. You describe the symptoms to the service manager and ask him or her to test the car for emissions.

As a result, you find out that the percentage of carbon monoxide coming from the tailpipe is in excess of the level allowed by law.

Perhaps the trouble is traced to a malfunctioning electronic engine control module or oxygen sensor, which are emissions control system parts. If so, the repair falls under the provisions of the emissions control systems warranty. You won't have to pay a penny for the repair, which incidentally would have cost you over $500. The repair also stops the bucking.

In this case, the key to the free repair was associating a driveability problem with an excessive emissions problem. Remember, the key to improving your chances of having your car fixed free is to bring the car to the service department of a dealership, to a state or municipal inspection station (if your state or municipality requires periodic emissions testing), or to a mechanic who has the proper equipment to test cars for excessive emissions.

The advantage of bringing the car to a dealer is that you won't be charged for the emissions test if the cause of the problem is a part or system that comes under the provisions of the emissions control systems warranty. According to the Clean Air Act, warranty work must be done by a "representative of the manufacturer" (that's a dealer) free of charge. Under the emissions control systems warranty, the full cost of troubleshooting and making a repair is to be assumed by the manufacturer. The car owner doesn't have to pay a penny unless the emissions test shows that the car is not emitting pollutants in excess of federal or state law.

Another advantage of having a dealer check the problem is that a service department can usually re-create the conditions that existed when the driveability problem occured, such as at a particular speed or engine temperature. Although state and municipal vehicle inspection stations usually don't charge for testing, it is difficult for them to re-create conditions. Independent mechanics may be able to do so, but they will probably charge to do the test, whether or not the cause of the problem turns out to be an emissions systems defect.

If testing is done by a state or municipal inspection station or an independent mechanic and your car fails the emissions test, be sure to get a copy of the results plus an explanation of why it failed. You will need this in order to have the free repair made by a dealer.

A CLOSER LOOK AT THE EMISSIONS SYSTEMS WARRANTY

The design and defect part of the emissions systems warranty remains in effect for five years or 50,000 miles, whichever occurs first, from the day that a new car takes to the road. The performance part of the emissions systems warranty is in effect for two years or 24,000 miles, whichever occurs first. (Exception: In California, the time/mileage period of the design and defect provision exceeds federal standards, remaining in effect for seven years or 70,000 miles, whichever occurs first, and the time/mileage period of the performance warranty remains in effect for three years or 50,000 miles, whichever occurs first.)

As long as the period of time or mileage has not expired, neither design and defect nor performance provisions terminate if the car is sold or given to another party. They are automatically transferred at no cost to the second, third, fourth, etc., owner until the time or mileage terms end.

Federal law states that if an original equipment component or system of your car fails because of faulty design or a defect in materials or workmanship and the failure causes the car to exceed federal emissions standards, the manufacturer must repair or replace the defective part or system free of charge for a period of five years or 50,000 miles, whichever occurs first. There is no cost to you—not for diagnosis, not for parts, not for labor.

The design and defect provision applies to the failure of all parts and systems of a vehicle whose primary purpose is to keep emissions at or below federal or state standards. Some of these parts and systems include the catalytic converter, exhaust gas recirculation system, positive crankcase ventilation system, early fuel evaporative system, and air injection system.

However, there are a slew of other parts and systems that many owners don't often associate with emissions control. When one of them fails, the unknowledgeable car owner may pay for a repair that could have been made free. Chief among these parts and systems are the electronic engine control module (computer) and all sensors, electronic ignition system, fuel injection system including fuel injectors, oxygen sensor, electronic choke, thermostatically controlled air cleaner, exhaust manifold, intake manifold, spark plugs, spark plug cables, turbochargers, and even the fuel tank cap and fuel tank. In addition, all bulbs, hoses, clamps, brackets, tubes, gaskets, seals, belts, connectors, fuel lines, and wiring harnesses that are used with all of these components are also covered.

Failure of almost all of these parts and systems will cause problems other than excessive emissions. If a test shows that emissions exceed legal standards, you can have the repair made for free. In most instances, that repair will not only lower the level of emissions; it will also resolve other problems.

WHAT YOU SHOULD KNOW ABOUT THE PERFORMANCE PROVISION

Federal law requires that for the first two years or 24,000 miles, whichever occurs first, the manufacturer must pay for all repairs required for your vehicle to pass a state- or municipality-mandated emissions test, no matter what the reason. In California, state law requires repair of a car that fails to pass a "smog" test for the first three years or 50,000 miles, whichever occurs first. There is no cost to the car owner—not for diagnosis, not for parts, not for labor—as long as certain conditions are met:

- You haven't misused, misfueled, or tampered with any emissions control part.
- You present to a representative of the manufacturer (i.e., the dealer) evidence of having failed an emissions test. In other words, get it in writing.

OTHER IMPORTANT FACTS

There are other facts about the emissions control systems warranty that you may find useful in getting a driveability problem resolved free of charge:

- Parts that the manufacturer says have to be replaced at a specific interval are covered only up to that replacement period, not necessarily for five years or 50,000 miles, whichever occurs first. For instance, if the spark plugs in your new car fail at 25,000 miles, producing excessive exhaust emissions, as well as engine misfire, and the manufacturer calls for their replacement at 30,000 miles, you would be entitled to a new set of plugs free of charge. But if you keep the plugs in use beyond 30,000 miles and they fail, you have to pay for another set.

- If an emissions control systems component goes bad (resulting in a poor driveability condition) because you failed to have scheduled maintenance performed, your claim for a free repair can be denied. Maintenance of a vehicle is your responsibility. However, if you have maintained your vehicle properly and are denied a free repair, get the reason for that denial in writing. Also, get the names of those involved—for example, the service department manager, dealership mechanic who worked on the car, and/or the manufacturer's regional or zone representative who becomes involved in the case. Refer to the owner's manual and warranty information booklet to determine whom you should contact at the manufacturer's headquarters to appeal the denial. If the matter isn't resolved to your satisfaction, present your case to the Warranty Complaint Department, Field Operation and Support Division (EN-397F), U.S. Environmental Protection Agency, 401 M Street SW, Washington, DC 20460.

"FRINGE" BENEFIT WARRANTIES

In addition to the warranties discussed thus far, new cars also come with tire and battery warranties. Tires are covered by the tire manufacturer, not by the new car manufacturer. This warranty usually states that a tire that fails because of a manufacturing deficiency or a flaw in material during the first 25 percent of usable tread wear or within 12 months from the day the tire is put into use will be replaced at no cost. Thereafter, you must share the cost on what is called a "prorated adjustment basis." For instance, if a tire had an original tread of 8/32 of an inch but has only 4/32 of an inch remaining when it fails, you must share the cost of a new tire on a 50/50 prorated adjustment basis with the tire company. You pay half; the tire company pays half.

A battery warranty works the same way. The car manufacturer will replace a defective battery without charge if it fails during the first 12 months or 12,000 miles, whichever occurs first. Thereafter, the cost of replacement is shared on a prorated adjustment basis.

In those cars that have air bags, the air bag (supplemental restraint) system is covered in full for at least three years regardless of mileage. This warranty is automatically transferred with the car at no cost if it is sold to another party.

Car manufacturers also issue corrosion warranties. Most manufacturers will repair or replace, at no cost to you, any metal panel that is completely rusted through (perforated). Surface rust doesn't count.

DEALING WITH A STUBBORN DEALER

Since manufacturers use them as a selling device, warranties other than those covering emissions control systems and air bag systems differ from manufacturer to manufacturer. As soon as one manufacturer changes the rules of the game, trying to get a leg up on the competition, others revise their warranties to stay competitive. Therefore, to get your car fixed free or nearly free under the terms of the warranties that come with it, you must read and understand those warranties. They are described in the warranty information booklet that comes with the car.

A warranty is a contract between you and the manufacturer. The dealer is merely a go-between. If your dealer denies a claim, you should not be discouraged. The dealer doesn't have the final word; the manufacturer does.

Car manufacturers acknowledge there are dealers who may assume too much authority. General Motors, for example, issued a Warranty Claims Procedure and Administration Bulletin to its dealers in April 1992 stating:

"Customer perceptions as a result of a warranty repair experience directly impacts customer satisfaction, loyalty, and repeat business to your dealership. Owners are particularly sensitive to service charges in conjunction with warranty repairs and generally do not expect to receive charges for repairs covered by the new vehicle and emissions warranties. Customers are not to be charged (except for the deductible provisions) for diagnosis in conjunction with warranty repairs under the new vehicle and emissions warranties."

Remember: The dealer is reimbursed by the manufacturer for a warranty repair. Therefore, if a dealer offhandedly denies a claim, telling you that it is not covered by warranty, don't automatically buy the argument. The only party who can deny a claim is the manufacturer.

If you and a dealer cannot come to an agreement, insist that a meeting be arranged with a technical representative from the manufacturer's zone, region, or district office. At that meeting, discuss the problem you are having with the car and which provision of which warranty you believe entitles you to a free repair. The representative may want to test the vehicle, so have it available.

If the dealer doesn't comply with your request to establish a meeting with the manufacturer's representative, do it yourself. The address and telephone number of the zone, region, or district office nearest you should be listed in your owner's manual. If not, write or phone the manufacturer's customer or warranty service department (see Appendix I).

It is important for you to keep complete written records of transactions between yourself, the dealer, and the manufacturer's field representative. This cannot be stressed enough. Documentation serves as proof that you followed the rules, that a dealer or manufacturer's representative wasn't able to solve a problem, and/or that what you thought was a claim under the provisions of one of the warranties hasn't been honored. Documents must show the date of service or attempted repair, mileage of the vehicle, description of the vehicle including the vehicle identification number, and explanation as to what transpired. Have this documentation transcribed on a service order form showing the name and address of the dealership, and have it signed and dated by all those involved in the case.

KEEPING YOUR PART OF THE BARGAIN

For the manufacturer to keep its part of the bargain under the terms of the warranty and fix your car for free, you must assume some responsibilities, which are as follows:

- You must not cause damage to the vehicle through alteration, misuse, or accident. Furthermore, you cannot expect the manufacturer to pay for damage caused by environmental conditions. Examples include damage caused by collision, fire, theft, vandalism, driving over curbs, overloading the vehicle, racing, tampering with an emissions system, using contaminated or improper fuels and fluids, exposure to the elements, hail, bird droppings, road salt, tree sap, flying stones, earthquake, flood, or windstorm.
- You must not cause damage by installing parts in the vehicle that are not authorized for use by the manufacturer. To be 100 percent safe, therefore, ask any technician who works on your car to use parts that bear the name of the vehicle manufacturer or substitute parts that are acceptable to the manufacturer.

Often, substitute parts manufactured by nationally known companies are acceptable, but not always. So be careful. An example of this is the oil filter authorized by Toyota for use in some of its engines. Toyota recommends that only an oil filter carrying the Toyota name be used—not even one made by any of the well-known oil filter manufacturers should be used.

Read your owner's manual. It's the only way to know whether you are safe in using parts made by companies other than the manufacturer of your car. Remember: Using a part that is not authorized is reason enough for a warranty claim (other than an emissions systems warranty claim) to be denied.

- Parts and services needed to keep the vehicle in sound condition, and parts that are subjected to normal wear and tear, are not normally covered by warranty. Thus, they are not replaced free of charge. Owners usually must pay for such things as oil changes, cleaning and polishing of the vehicle, tire rotation, lubricants and fluids, engine tune-ups, filters, windshield wiper blades, brake pads or linings, and clutch linings. Some manufacturers, however, provide extended warranty coverage that includes routine maintenance and replacement of worn parts.
- You must not cause damage to the vehicle by failing to maintain it in accordance with instructions in the maintenance schedule. Misinterpretation of a maintenance schedule is not an excuse. It's in this area that many car owners falter, which results in warranty claims being denied by manufacturers.

UNDERSTANDING MAINTENANCE SCHEDULES

Manufacturers provide two maintenance schedules: a maintenance schedule for "normal" operation of your car and a maintenance schedule for "severe" operation. These schedules are described in owners' manuals or in maintenance and warranty booklets given to owners when they purchase their new vehicles. Selecting the wrong maintenance schedule (the terms are often misinterpreted) can result in a manufacturer's denying a warranty claim and causing a car owner to pay for a repair that would have otherwise been paid for by the manufacturer.

Although a car owner may believe he or she is driving a vehicle under "normal" conditions, that may not be the case. For example, driving a car once a day on an interstate highway at 55 or 60 mph for only two miles is not considered normal operation. It is categorized as severe operation. Examples of other severe types of operations include driving a car daily in New York City or driving at 60 mph from Fort Lauderdale to Naples every day in temperatures above 90°F.

To be on the safe side, when selecting which maintenance schedule to use, interpret the term "normal operation" as meeting only the following criteria: driving a car primarily (that is, most of the year) for at least 10 miles a day in an environment that is free of dust and industrial emissions at a steady rate of speed above 50 mph in a region where the ambient temperature stays between 32°F and 90°F. To be on the safe side and safeguard your rights to free repairs, all other primary driving conditions should be considered severe, in which case the car should be serviced according to the severe operation maintenance schedule. Included in the definition of the term "severe operation" are the following conditions:

• If most trips are less than 10 miles.
• If the vehicle is used in stop-and-go traffic that causes the engine to idle or run at low speeds more often than not.
• If the car is operated when the ambient temperature is consistently below 32°F or above 90°F for more than a month at a time.
• If the vehicle is driven in a dusty or industrialized region.
• If the car is used to tow a trailer.

Usually the severe operation maintenance schedule calls for servicing the vehicle at one-half the time/mileage period called for by the normal operation maintenance schedule. Thus, if the normal operation maintenance schedule calls for servicing the engine every six months or 7,500 miles, whichever occurs first, the severe operation maintenance schedule will call for maintenance every three months or 3,750 miles, whichever occurs first.

Again, documentation showing that you have been conscientious about maintaining your car properly can be important when you put in a claim for a free repair under the terms of a warranty. For example, to have the manufacturer replace a camshaft (if this very expensive part should fail) under the warranty, you will probably need written proof that you have changed engine oil every three months or 3,750 miles as called for by the severe maintenance schedule.

RESOLVING WARRANTY DISPUTES

Each new car warranty is a contract between the buyer and the manufacturer. As with most legal agreements, it contains "ifs, ands, and buts." For example, if the car owner violates the terms of the warranty by not doing something called for, such as not changing the engine oil, the contract may become null and void should the engine seize. On the other hand, if the car owner believes the manufacturer has violated the terms of the warranty by not, for instance, rendering a free repair due the owner, then the owner has several avenues to seek recourse.

You can take the manufacturer to court, but this is a serious course of action and is often not necessary. It is also expensive, because you can lose the case and have to pay all legal fees. If you win the case, however, then the manufacturer will have to pay to fix the car, all legal fees, and the cost of repairing any damage the vehicle suffered as a result of the manufacturer's not repairing it sooner.

There are two less-drastic, inexpensive, and usually productive courses of action to follow before deciding to pursue legal action: using the customer arbitration program; or following a state warranty enforcement law procedure, which is commonly referred to as a lemon law. Most states have now adopted lemon laws.

Each of these programs has a different purpose. The purpose of customer arbitration programs is to mediate warranty disputes. The purpose of lemon laws is to provide relief for customers whose cars cannot be repaired after several attempts. The exact number varies from state to state, but three is the norm.

WHAT TO DO FIRST

Most disputes over who is responsible for paying the cost of a repair can be settled amicably by following this procedure:

1. If you and a dealership service representative differ as to who is responsible for paying for a repair, take the matter up with the owner of the dealership or with someone who had been authorized to act in the owner's behest, such as the new car sales manager.

2. If the owner of the dealership or his or her representative agrees with the service representative that you are responsible for payment and the repair has already been made, write a check or use a credit card for the repair so you have documentation. Keep a record of the transaction, including a written explanation of why your claim was denied.

3. Request that a meeting be set up with a field representative of the manufacturer. State your case. If the manufacturer's field representative comes down on the side of the dealership and refutes your claim, or if he or she offers a partial payment that isn't to your liking, send a certified letter (return receipt requested) to the Customer Relations Department of the manufacturer at the address of the manufacturer's district office or headquarters listed in Appendix I. Send copies of all the documentation—from the time you voiced your complaint to the service representative up to the present. You will need these documents if you have to take the matter to a customer or state arbitration panel or to court.

4. If contacting the manufacturer's district office or headquarters doesn't settle the matter, it is time to begin the arbitration process.

THE CUSTOMER ARBITRATION PROCEDURE

Arbitration is the process by which two parties—in this case, you and the manufacturer of your car—authorize a third party to resolve a dispute. The third party used by most manufacturers is the Better Business Bureau (BBB) AUTO LINE, or the Automotive Consumer Action Program (AUTOCAP) of the National Automobile Dealers Association. The address for AUTO LINE is BBB AUTO LINE, Council of Better Business Bureaus, 4200 Wilson Boulevard, Suite 800, Arlington, VA 22203. The toll-free telephone number is 800-955-5100. The address for AUTO-CAP is AUTOCAP, National Automobile Dealers Association, 8400 Westpark Drive, McLean, VA 22102. The telephone number is 703-821-7000.

Some manufacturers, particularly Chrysler and Ford, don't use AUTO LINE or AUTOCAP but have set up their own arbitration panels. This may give the appearance of asking the fox to guard the henhouse, but this is not the case. Both Chrysler and Ford arbitration panels are free to act as independently of the manufacturer and its dealers as are AUTO LINE and AUTOCAP.

As with AUTO LINE and AUTOCAP, the panels that sit in judgment of disputes with Chrysler and Ford consist of three voting members: a local consumer advocate, an independent technical representative certified by the National Institute of Automotive Service Excellence, and a representative from the general public.

In addition to avoiding the hassle of going to court, there are these other benefits associated with customer arbitration:

- It's free. You don't need a lawyer, unless you want one, and there isn't any fee for filing a complaint.
- It's relatively fast. In most cases, a decision will be given within 40 days from the time you file your complaint.
- You need not attend the meeting at which your case is discussed unless you wish to appear. However, you do have to submit a written statement of your complaint, which has to include your name, address, a description of the vehicle, and the vehicle identification number. Offer any documentation you believe is necessary to strengthen your case.
- The panel's decision is binding on the dealer but not on you. You don't have to accept it. If you wish to pursue further action, you can bring the matter to court.

Important: Keep in mind that customer arbitration panels review only warranty disputes. They don't handle matters involving the sale of vehicles, personal injury, property damage, design of a vehicle, or matters in litigation.

LEMON LAWS

Each state that has a warranty enforcement (lemon) law has its own procedure to follow. All of the laws provide for replacement or repurchase by the manufacturer of a vehicle that has a defect that cannot be repaired after several attempts. Currently, the following states have warranty enforcement laws on the books: California, Colorado, Connecticut, Florida, Georgia, Hawaii, Illinois, Indiana, Iowa, Kentucky, Maine, Maryland, Massachusetts, Minnesota, Missouri, Montana, New Hampshire, New Jersey, New Mexico, New York, North Carolina, Ohio, Pennsylvania, South Carolina, Vermont, Virginia, and West Virginia. A law is also in effect in the District of Columbia.

You can write or call for a description of the law adopted in your state and for an explanation of how to file a claim. See Appendix II for the applicable address and phone number.

EXTENDED WARRANTIES

According to federal law, "extended warranties" that are usually offered by salespeople to buyers of new and used cars are *not* warranties. They are auto service contracts.

A warranty is a written promise by the manufacturer that the car that you are buying will perform up to stipulated standards. Warranties automatically come with new cars. You don't have to buy them.

On the other hand, you pay extra for an auto service contract. Many auto service contracts are not backed by the manufacturers of the vehicles but by independent companies, some of which in the past have not remained in business for the full terms of the contracts. Furthermore, many of the failures that an auto service contract covers duplicate what a warranty covers. For example, why pay for protection against engine failure for the six years or 60,000 miles provided by an auto service contract when the powertrain or bumper-to-bumper warranty that automatically comes with the car protects you against engine failure for seven years or 70,000 miles, whichever comes first.

Ironically, the same salesperson who extols the manufacturer's warranty when he or she is trying to sell you a new car will turn around and try to sell you on the virtues of an extended "warranty" when you agree to buy the new car. Auto service contracts are big moneymakers for dealerships.

KNOW YOUR RIGHTS WHEN BUYING A USED CAR

When you shop for a car at the used car department of a new car dealer or at an independent used car dealer's establishment, look for the buyer's guide sticker that is posted on the window of the car. This sticker, which is required by the Federal Trade Commission, will inform you whether the car is being sold with a carryover new car warranty, with a warranty issued by the used car dealer, with an implied warranty, or "as is."

Carryover New Car Warranty. If any of the new car warranties are still in effect and can be transferred to a buyer, ask how much it will cost. If you are lucky, the manufacturer or the dealer may cover the cost of the transfer.

Note: Don't forget that the emissions system and supplemental inflatable restraint system warranties are automatically transferred at no cost.

Used Car Dealer Warranty. When a dealer offers a written warranty on a car, it must be stipulated what systems or components the warranty covers and whether coverage is full or limited. A *full* warranty will provide the following terms and conditions:

- Warranty service will be provided to whoever owns the vehicle during the warranty period.
- Warranty service will be provided free of charge.
- At your choice, the dealer will provide either a replacement or a full refund if the dealer isn't able to repair the system or component covered by the warranty after a reasonable number of attempts.

- Warranty service is provided as a precondition for receiving service and doesn't require you to do anything to receive service except to notify the dealer.

If any of these items is not included in the written warranty, then it is not a full warranty; it is a limited warranty.

Most used car dealer warranties are limited in scope, which means that there are some costs and responsibilities the buyer has to assume. When a warranty is limited in scope, according to law, the dealer must provide the following information on the buyer's guide sticker:

1. The percentage of the repair cost that the dealer will assume, and the percentage you will have to assume
2. The specific parts and systems that are covered by the warranty
3. The duration of the warranty for each part and system that is covered by the warranty.

Implied Warranty. An implied warranty is neither written nor spoken. It is based on the principle that a seller of a car will stand behind the product. Implied warranties are in effect in every state and come with the purchase of a used car unless the dealer states in writing that implied warranties do not exist—for example, by using such phrases as "as is" or "sold with all faults."

The so-called "warranty of merchantability" is the most common type of implied warranty. It refers to the fact that the seller promises the product will do what it is supposed to do. In the case of a car, the implied warranty of merchantability promises that the car will run. If it doesn't run, the dealer is obliged by law to fix it free of charge.

The other type of implied warranty is called the "warranty of purpose," meaning the product will fulfill the purpose for which it is being sold. For instance, if you buy a pickup truck with the understanding that the truck will haul no less than a specific amount of cargo, then the truck must be able to do that or the dealer can be required to repair the truck—for example, by installing overload shock absorbers and new springs. Don't rely on a dealer's word that the vehicle will fulfill its purpose. Get every claim in writing.

As Is (Without a Warranty). If the buyer's guide sticker on a used car indicates "as is," it means that there aren't any express or implied warranties that come with the vehicle. Therefore, the dealer can't be held responsible for making any repairs or modifications.

Some states do not permit "as-is" sales of used cars. They are Connecticut, Kansas, Maine, Maryland, Massachusetts, Minnesota, Mississippi, New York, Rhode Island, Vermont, and West Virginia—also the District of Columbia.

Used cars sold by private parties are not subject to any law and are not covered by any implied warranties demanded by the state. You are on your own unless the party selling the car stipulates in writing that he or she will stand behind the car and, if so, to what extent and for how long. However, it may be possible to transfer to you any new car warranties that are still in effect. To find out if this is possible, ask to see the warranties, get in touch with the manufacturer, or call a dealer who sells vehicles of the same make.

Note: Don't forget that the emissions system and air bag system warranties are automatically transferred at no cost.

APPENDIX I

CAR MANUFACTURERS

If you have a problem with a new car, try to reach an agreement with the dealer. If you are not successful, contact the manufacturer's regional or national office listed in this section. Send letters to the director of customer relations.

If you wish to call, telephone numbers (some, toll-free) are provided. All of the toll-free national headquarters numbers can be dialed from anywhere in the continental United States. A regional office toll-free number is valid only in the state listed.

ACURA

1919 Torrance Boulevard
Torrance, CA 90501-2746
800-382-2238

ALFA-ROMEO DISTRIBUTORS OF NORTH AMERICA, INC.

8259 Exchange Drive
P.O. Box 598026
Orlando, FL 32859-8026
407-856-5000

AMERICAN HONDA MOTOR COMPANY, INC.

ALABAMA, FLORIDA, GEORGIA, TENNESSEE

1500 Morrison Parkway
Alpharetta, GA 30201-2199
404-442-2045 (collect calls accepted)

ALASKA, HAWAII, IDAHO, MONTANA, NORTH DAKOTA, OREGON, SOUTH DAKOTA, WASHINGTON, WYOMING

12439 N.E. Airport Way
Portland, OR 97220-0186
503-256-0943

ARIZONA, COLORADO, KANSAS, NEBRASKA, NEVADA, NEW MEXICO, OKLAHOMA, TEXAS (El Paso), UTAH

1600 South Abilene Street, Suite D
Aurora, CO 80012-5815
303-696-3935

ARKANSAS (excluding Fayetteville, Bentonville, Fort Smith, Jonesboro), LOUISIANA, MISSISSIPPI, OKLAHOMA (Lawton, Ardmore), TEXAS (excluding El Paso)

4529 Royal Lane
Irving, TX 75063-2583
214-929-5481

CALIFORNIA

700 Van Ness Avenue
Torrance, CA 90509-2260
310-781-4565

CONNECTICUT (Fairfield County), DELAWARE, NEW JERSEY, NEW YORK (New York City and its five boroughs, Long Island, Westchester County), OHIO (Steubenville), PENNSYLVANIA, WEST VIRGINIA (Wheeling)

115 Gaither Drive
Moorestown, NJ 08057-0337
609-235-5533

CONNECTICUT (excluding Fairfield County), MAINE, MASSACHUSETTS, NEW HAMPSHIRE, NEW YORK STATE (excluding New York City and its five boroughs, Long Island, Westchester County), RHODE ISLAND, VERMONT

555 Old County Road
Windsor Locks, CT 06096-0465
203-623-3310

DISTRICT OF COLUMBIA, MARYLAND, NORTH CAROLINA, SOUTH CAROLINA, VIRGINIA, WEST VIRGINIA

902 Wind River Lane, Suite 200
Gaithersburg, MD 20878-1974
301-990-2020

ILLINOIS, IOWA, MICHIGAN (Upper Peninsula), MINNESOTA, MISSOURI, WISCONSIN

601 Campus Drive, Suite A-9
Arlington Heights, IL 60004-1407
708-870-5600

INDIANA, KENTUCKY, MICHIGAN (except for Upper Peninsula), OHIO

101 South Stanfield Road
Troy, OH 45373-8010
513-332-6250

CORPORATE OFFICE

1919 Torrance Boulevard
Torrance, CA 90501-2746
310-783-3260

AMERICAN ISUZU MOTORS, INC.

ALABAMA, FLORIDA, GEORGIA, MISSISSIPPI, NORTH CAROLINA, SOUTH CAROLINA

205 Hembree Park Drive
Roswell, GA 30076
404-475-1995

ALASKA, COLORADO, HAWAII, IDAHO, MONTANA, NEBRASKA, NEVADA (northern), OREGON, SOUTH DAKOTA, UTAH, WASHINGTON, WYOMING

8727 148th Avenue, N.E.
Redmond, WA 98052
206-881-0203

ARIZONA, ARKANSAS, KANSAS, LOUISIANA, NEVADA (southern), NEW MEXICO, OKLAHOMA, TEXAS

1150 Isuzu Parkway
Grand Prairie, TX 75050
214-647-2911

CALIFORNIA

One Autry Street
Irvine, CA 92718-2785
714-770-2626

CONNECTICUT, MAINE, MASSACHUSETTS, NEW HAMPSHIRE, NEW JERSEY (north of Toms River), NEW YORK, RHODE ISLAND, VERMONT

156 Ludlow Avenue
P.O. Box 965
Northvale, NJ 07647-0965
201-784-1414

DELAWARE, KENTUCKY, MARYLAND, NEW JERSEY (south of Toms River), PENNSYLVANIA, TENNESSEE, VIRGINIA, WEST VIRGINIA

One Isuzu Way
Glen Burnie, MD 21061
410-761-2121

ILLINOIS, INDIANA, IOWA, MICHIGAN, MINNESOTA, MISSOURI, NORTH DAKOTA, OHIO, WISCONSIN

1820 Jarvis Avenue
Elk Grove Village, IL 60007
708-952-8111

HEADQUARTERS

13181 Crossroads Parkway North
P.O. Box 2480
City of Industry, CA 91746-0480
310-699-0500
800-255-6727

AMERICAN SUZUKI MOTOR CORPORATION

3251 E. Imperial Highway
Brea, CA 92622-6722
714-996-7040

AUDI OF AMERICA, INC.

CONNECTICUT, NEW JERSEY, NEW YORK

125 South Greenbush Road
Orangeburg, NY 10962
914-578-5000

ALL OTHER STATES: CORPORATE OFFICE

3800 Hamlin Road
Auburn Hills, MI 48326
800-822-2834

BMW OF NORTH AMERICA, INC.

ALABAMA, ARKANSAS, FLORIDA, GEORGIA, LOUISIANA, MISSISSIPPI, NORTH CAROLINA, OKLAHOMA, SOUTH CAROLINA, TENNESSEE, TEXAS (except El Paso), VIRGINIA (except northern)

1280 Hightower Trail
Atlanta, GA 30350-2977
404-552-3800

ALASKA, ARIZONA, CALIFORNIA, COLORADO, HAWAII, IDAHO, MONTANA, NEVADA, NEW MEXICO, OREGON, TEXAS (El Paso), UTAH, WASHINGTON, WYOMING

12541 Beatrice Street
P.O. Box 66916
Los Angeles, CA 90066
310-574-7300

CONNECTICUT, DELAWARE, MAINE, MARYLAND, MASSACHUSETTS, NEW JERSEY, NEW HAMPSHIRE, NEW YORK, PENNSYLVANIA, RHODE ISLAND, VERMONT, VIRGINIA (northern), WASHINGTON, D.C., WEST VIRGINIA

1 BMW Plaza
Montvale, NJ 07645
201-573-2100

ILLINOIS, INDIANA, IOWA, KANSAS, KENTUCKY, MICHIGAN, MINNESOTA, MISSOURI, NEBRASKA, NORTH DAKOTA, OHIO, SOUTH DAKOTA, WISCONSIN

498 East Commerce Drive
Schaumburg, IL 60173
708-310-2700

CORPORATE OFFICE

P.O. Box 1227
Westwood, NJ 07675-1227
201-307-4000

CHRYSLER MOTORS CORPORATION

ATLANTA ZONE OFFICE

3350 Cumberland Circle
Atlanta, GA 30339
404-644-6823

BOSTON ZONE OFFICE

550 Forbes Boulevard
Mansfield, MA 02048-2038
508-261-2299

CHARLOTTE ZONE OFFICE

4944 Parkway Plaza Boulevard, Suite 470
Charlotte, NC 28217
704-357-7065

CHICAGO ZONE OFFICE

650 Warrenville Road, Suite 502
Lisle, IL 60532
708-515-2450

CINCINNATI ZONE OFFICE

P.O. Box 41902
Cincinnati, OH 45241
513-530-1500

DALLAS ZONE OFFICE

P.O. Box 110162
Carrollton, TX 75011-0162
214-242-8462

DENVER ZONE OFFICE

12225 E. 39th Avenue
Denver, CO 80239
303-373-8853

DETROIT ZONE OFFICE

P.O. Box 3000
Troy, MI 48007-3000
313-952-1300

HOUSTON ZONE OFFICE

363 North Sam Houston Parkway East,
    Suite 590
Houston, TX 77060-2405
713-820-7062

KANSAS CITY ZONE OFFICE

P.O. Box 25668
Overland Park, KS 66210-5668
913-469-3090

LOS ANGELES ZONE OFFICE

1100 Town and Country Road, Suite 200
P.O. Box 14112
Orange, CA 92668-4600
714-565-5111

MEMPHIS ZONE OFFICE

P.O. Box 18008
Memphis, TN 38181-0008
901-797-3870

MILWAUKEE ZONE OFFICE

P.O. Box 1634
Waukesha, WI 53187-1634
414-798-3750

MINNEAPOLIS ZONE OFFICE

P.O. Box 1231
Minneapolis, MN 55440
612-553-2546

NEW ORLEANS ZONE OFFICE

P.O. Box 157
Metairie, LA 70004
504-830-3400

NEW YORK ZONE OFFICE

500 Route 303
Tappan, NY 10983-1592
914-359-0110

ORLANDO ZONE OFFICE

8000 South Orange Blossom Trail
Orlando, FL 32809
407-352-7402

PHILADELPHIA ZONE OFFICE

Valley Brook Corporate Center
101 Linden Wood Drive, Suite 320
Malvern, PA 19355
215-251-2990

PHOENIX ZONE OFFICE

11811 No. Tatum Boulevard, Suite 4025
Phoenix, AZ 85028
602-494-6899

PITTSBURGH ZONE OFFICE

Penn Center West 3, Suite 420
Pittsburgh, PA 15276
412-788-6622

PORTLAND ZONE OFFICE

P.O. Box 744
Beaverton, OR 97075
503-526-5555

SAN FRANCISCO ZONE OFFICE

6150 Zone Ridge Mall, Suite 200
P.O. Box 5009
Pleasanton, CA 94588-0509
415-463-1770

ST. LOUIS ZONE OFFICE

P.O. Box 278
Hazelwood, MO 63042
314-895-0731

SYRACUSE ZONE OFFICE

P.O. Box 603
DeWitt, NY 13214-0603
315-445-6941

WASHINGTON, D.C., ZONE OFFICE

P.O. Box 1900
Bowie, MD 20717
301-464-4040

CORPORATE OFFICE

P.O. Box 32
Center Line, MI 48015-9302
800-992-1997

FERRARI NORTH AMERICA, INC.

CORPORATE OFFICE

250 Sylvan Avenue
Englewood Cliffs, NJ 07632
201-816-2650

FORD MOTOR COMPANY

CORPORATE OFFICE

300 Renaissance Center
P.O. Box 43360
Detroit, MI 48243
800-392-3673 (all models except Lincoln and Merkur)
800-521-4140 (Lincoln and Merkur only)

GENERAL MOTORS CORPORATION

Customer Assistance Center
Buick Motor Division
902 East Hamilton Avenue
Flint, MI 48550
800-521-7300

Consumer Relations Center
Cadillac Motor Car Division
3009 Van Dyke
Warren, MI 48090-9025
800-458-8006

Customer Assistance Center
Chevrolet/Geo Motor Division
P.O. Box 7047
Troy, MI 48007-7047
800-222-1020

Customer Service Department
GMC Truck Division
Mail Code 1606-03
31 East Judson Street
Pontiac, MI 48342-2230
800-462-8782

Customer Assistance Network
Oldsmobile Division
P.O. Box 30095
Lansing, MI 48909-7595
800-442-6537

Customer Assistance Center
Pontiac Division
One Pontiac Plaza, Room 317B
Pontiac, MI 48340-2952
800-762-2737

Saturn Assistance Center
Saturn Corporation
P.O. Box 1500
100 Saturn Parkway
Spring Hill, TN 37174-1500
800-553-6000

HYUNDAI MOTOR AMERICA

10550 Talbert Avenue
P.O. Box 20850
Fountain Valley, CA 92728-0850
800-633-5151

JAGUAR CARS, INC.

555 MacArthur Boulevard
Mahwah, NJ 07430-2327
201-818-8500

MAZDA MOTOR OF AMERICA, INC.

CORPORATE HEADQUARTERS

P.O. Box 19734
Irvine, CA 92713
800-222-5500

MERCEDES-BENZ OF NORTH AMERICA, INC.

NATIONAL HEADQUARTERS

One Mercedes Drive
Montvale, NJ 07645-0350
201-573-0600

MITSUBISHI MOTOR SALES OF AMERICA, INC.

CORPORATE OFFICE

6400 Katella Avenue
Cypress, CA 90630-0064
800-222-0037

NISSAN MOTOR CORPORATION IN USA

CORPORATE OFFICE

P.O. Box 191
Gardena, CA 90248-0191
800-647-7261

PORSCHE CARS NORTH AMERICA, INC.

100 West Liberty Street
P.O. Box 30911
Reno, NV 89520-3911
800-545-8039

SAAB CARS USA, INC.

P.O. Box 900
Norcross, GA 30091

SUBARU OF AMERICA

ALABAMA, FLORIDA, GEORGIA, MARYLAND, NORTH CAROLINA, SOUTH CAROLINA, TENNESSEE, VIRGINIA, WASHINGTON, D.C., WEST VIRGINIA

220 The Bluffs
Austell, GA 30001
404-732-3200

ALASKA, IDAHO, MONTANA, NEBRASKA, NORTH DAKOTA, OREGON, SOUTH DAKOTA, UTAH, WASHINGTON, WYOMING

8040 East 33rd Drive
Portland, OR 97211
800-878-6677

ARIZONA, CALIFORNIA, NEVADA

12A Whatney Drive
Irvine, CA 92718-2895
714-951-9264

ARKANSAS, COLORADO, KANSAS, MISSISSIPPI, NEW MEXICO, OKLAHOMA, TEXAS

15000 East 39th Avenue
Aurora, CO 80011
303-371-3820

CONNECTICUT, MAINE, MASSACHUSETTS, NEW HAMPSHIRE, RHODE ISLAND, VERMONT

95 Morse Street
Norwood, MA 02062
617-769-5100

DELAWARE, PENNSYLVANIA, SOUTHERN NEW JERSEY

1504 Glen Avenue
Moorestown, NJ 08057
609-234-7600

HAWAII

Schuman-Carriage Company, Inc.
1234 South Beretania Street
P.O. Box 2420
Honolulu, HI 96804
808-533-6211

ILLINOIS, INDIANA, IOWA, KENTUCKY, MICHIGAN, MINNESOTA, MISSOURI, OHIO, WISCONSIN

301 Mitchell Court
Addison, IL 60101
708-953-1188

NEW YORK, NORTHERN NEW JERSEY

6 Ramland Road
Orangeburg, NY 10962
914-359-2500

CORPORATE OFFICE

P.O. Box 6000
Cherry Hill, NJ 08034-6000
609-488-3278

TOYOTA MOTOR SALES, INC.

Customer Assistance Center
Department A102
19001 South Western Avenue
Torrance, CA 90509
800-331-4331

VOLKSWAGEN UNITED STATES, INC.

CONNECTICUT, NEW JERSEY, NEW YORK

125 South Greenbush Road
Orangeburg, NY 10962
914-578-5000
800-822-8987

ALL OTHER STATES

Consumer Relations
3800 Hamlin Road
Auburn Hills, MI 48326
800-822-8987

VOLVO CARS OF NORTH AMERICA

CORPORATE OFFICE

15 Volvo Drive, Building D
P.O. Box 914
Rockleigh NJ 07647-0914
201-767-4737

APPENDIX II

WHOM TO CONTACT FOR STATE LEMON LAW INFORMATION

ALABAMA

Consumer Protection Division
Office of the Attorney General
11 South Union Street
Montgomery, AL 36130

ALASKA

Office of the Attorney General
Anchorage, AK 99500

ARIZONA

Consumer Protection
Office of the Attorney General
1275 West Washington Street
Phoenix, AZ 85007

ARKANSAS

Consumer Protection Division
Office of the Attorney General
200 Tower Building
323 Center Street
Little Rock, AR 72201

CALIFORNIA

Department of Consumer Affairs
400 R Street, Suite 1040
Sacramento, CA 95814

COLORADO

Consumer Protection Unit
Office of the Attorney General
110 16th Street, 10th Floor
Denver, CO 80202

CONNECTICUT

Department of Consumer
Protection
State Office Building
165 Capitol Avenue
Hartford, CT 06106

DELAWARE

Division of Consumer Affairs
Department of Community
Affairs
820 North French Street, 4th
Floor
Wilmington, DE 19801

DISTRICT OF COLUMBIA

Department of Consumer and
Regulatory Affairs
614 H Street, N.W.
Washington, DC 20001

FLORIDA

Department of Agriculture and
Consumer Services
Division of Consumer Services
218 Mayo Building
Tallahassee, FL 32399

GEORGIA

Governors Office of Consumer
Affairs
2 Martin Luther King, Jr. Drive,
S.E.
Atlanta, GA 30334

HAWAII

Office of Consumer Protection
Department of Commerce and
Consumer Affairs
828 Fort St. Mall, Suite 600B ·
P.O. Box 3767
Honolulu, HI 96812-3767

IDAHO

Office of the Attorney General
Consumer Protection Unit
Statehouse, Room 113A
Boise, ID 83720-1000

ILLINOIS

Governors Office of Citizens
Assistance
222 South College
Springfield, IL 62706

INDIANA

Consumer Protection Division
Office of the Attorney General
219 State House
Indianapolis, IN 46204

IOWA

Consumer Protection Division
Office of the Attorney General
1300 East Walnut Street, 2nd
Floor
Des Moines, IA 50319

KANSAS

Consumer Protection Division
Office of the Attorney General
301 West 10th
Kansas Judicial Center
Topeka, KS 66612-1597

KENTUCKY

Consumer Protection Division
Office of the Attorney General
209 Saint Clair Street
Frankfort, KY 40601-1875

LOUISIANA

Consumer Protection Section
Office of the Attorney General
State Capitol Building
P.O. Box 94005
Baton Rouge, LA 70804-9005

MAINE

Consumer and Antitrust Division
Office of the Attorney General
State House Station No. 6
Augusta, ME 04333

MARYLAND

Consumer Protection Division
Office of the Attorney General
200 St. Paul Place
Baltimore, MD 21202-2021

MASSACHUSETTS

Consumer Protection Division
Department of the Attorney
  general
131 Tremont Street
Boston, MA 02111

MICHIGAN

Consumer Protection Division
Office of the Attorney General
P.O. Box 30213
Lansing, MI 48909

MINNESOTA

Office of Consumer Services
Office of the Attorney General
117 University Avenue
St. Paul, MN 55155

MISSISSIPPI

Consumer Protection Division
Office of the Attorney General
P.O. Box 22947
Jackson, MS 39225-2947

MISSOURI

Office of the Attorney General
Consumer Complaints or
  Problems
P.O. Box 899
Jefferson City, MO 65102

MONTANA

Consumer Affairs Unit
Department of Commerce
1424 Ninth Avenue
Helena, MT 59620

NEBRASKA

Consumer Protection Division
Department of Justice
2115 State Capitol
P.O. Box 98920
Lincoln, NE 68509

NEVADA

Commissioner of Consumer
  Affairs
Department of Commerce
State Mail Room Complex
Las Vegas, NV 89158

NEW HAMPSHIRE

Consumer Protection and
  Antitrust Bureau
Office of the Attorney General
State House Annex
Concord, NH 03301

NEW JERSEY

Division of Consumer Affairs
P.O. Box 45027
Newark, NJ 07101

NEW MEXICO

Consumer Protection Division
Office of the Attorney General
P.O. Drawer 1508
Santa Fe, NM 87504

NEW YORK

New York State Consumer
   Protection Board
99 Washington Avenue
Albany, NY 12210-2891

NORTH CAROLINA

Consumer Protection Section
Office of the Attorney General
Raney Building
P.O. Box 629
Raleigh, NC 27602

NORTH DAKOTA

Office of the Attorney General
600 East Boulevard
Bismarck, ND 58505

OHIO

Office of the Attorney General
30 East Broad Street
State Office Tower, 25th Floor
Columbus, OH 43266-0410

OKLAHOMA

Office of the Attorney General
420 West Main, Suite 550
Oklahoma City, OK 73102

OREGON

Financial Fraud Section
Department of Justice
Justice Building
Salem, OR 97310

PENNSYLVANIA

Bureau of Consumer Protection
Office of the Attorney General

Strawberry Square, 14th Floor
Harrisburg, PA 17120

RHODE ISLAND

Consumer Protection Division
Office of the Attorney General
72 Pine Street
Providence, RI 02903

SOUTH CAROLINA

Office of the Attorney General
P.O. Box 11549
Columbia, SC 29211

SOUTH DAKOTA

Office of the Attorney General
500 East Capitol
State Capitol Building
Pierre, SD 57501-5070

TENNESSEE

Antitrust and Consumer
   Protection Division
Office of the Attorney General
450 James Robertson Parkway
Nashville, TN 37243-0485

TEXAS

Consumer Protection Division
Office of the Attorney General
P.O. Box 12548
Austin, TX 78711

UTAH

Division of Consumer Protection
Department of Commerce
160 East Third, South
P.O. Box 45802
Salt Lake City, UT 84145-0802

VERMONT

Office of the Attorney General
109 State Street
Montpelier, VT 05609-1001

VIRGINIA

Office of the Attorney General
Supreme Court Building
101 North Eighth Street
Richmond, VA 23219

WASHINGTON

Office of the Attorney General
111 Olympia Avenue, NE
Olympia, WA 98501

WEST VIRGINIA

Consumer Protection Division
Office of the Attorney General
812 Quarrier Street, 6th Floor
Charleston, WV 25301

WISCONSIN

Department of Agriculture, Trade
    and Consumer Protection
801 West Badger Road
P.O. Box 8911
Madison, WI 53708

WYOMING

Office of the Attorney General
123 State Capitol Building
Cheyenne, WY 82002

INDEX